How to Use This Book

Look for these special features in this book:

SIDEBARS, **CHARTS**, **GRAPHS**, and original **MAPS** expand your understanding of what's being discussed—and also make useful sources for classroom reports.

FAQs answer common **F**requently **A**sked **Q**uestions about people, places, and things.

WOW FACTORS offer "Who knew?" facts to keep you thinking.

TRAVEL GUIDE gives you tips on exploring the state—either in person or right from your chair!

PROJECT ROOM provides fun ideas for school assignments and incredible research projects. Plus, there's a guide to primary sources—what they are and how to cite them.

Please note: All statistics are as up-to-date as possible at the time of publication. Population data is taken from the 2010 census.

Consultants: William Loren Katz; James M. Robertson, Director and State Geologist, Wisconsin Geological and Natural History Survey; Chad Ronnander, Visiting Assistant Professor of History, University of Wisconsin–Eau Claire; Patricia Stovey, Assistant Professor of History, University of Wisconsin–La Crosse

Book production by The Design Lab

Library of Congress Cataloging-in-Publication Data
Blashfield, Jean F.
 Wisconsin / by Jean F. Blashfield. — Revised edition.
  pages cm. — (America, the beautiful. Third series)
 Includes bibliographical references and index.
 ISBN 978-0-531-24874-4 (lib. bdg.)
 1. Wisconsin—Juvenile literature. I. Title.
 F581.3.B58 2014
 977.5—dc23   2013033045

©2014, 2008 Scholastic Inc.
All rights reserved. Published in 2014 by Children's Press, an imprint of Scholastic Inc.
Printed in the United States of America 141
SCHOLASTIC, CHILDREN'S PRESS, and associated logos are trademarks and/or registered trademarks of Scholastic Inc.

1 2 3 4 5 6 7 8 9 10 R 23 22 21 20 19 18 17 16 15 14

Wisconsin

BY JEAN F. BLASHFIELD

Third Series, Revised Edition

Children's Press®
An Imprint of Scholastic Inc.
New York ★ Toronto ★ London ★ Auckland ★ Sydney
Mexico City ★ New Delhi ★ Hong Kong
Danbury, Connecticut

CONTENTS

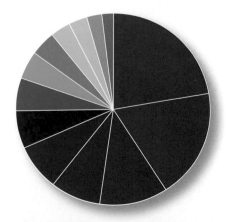

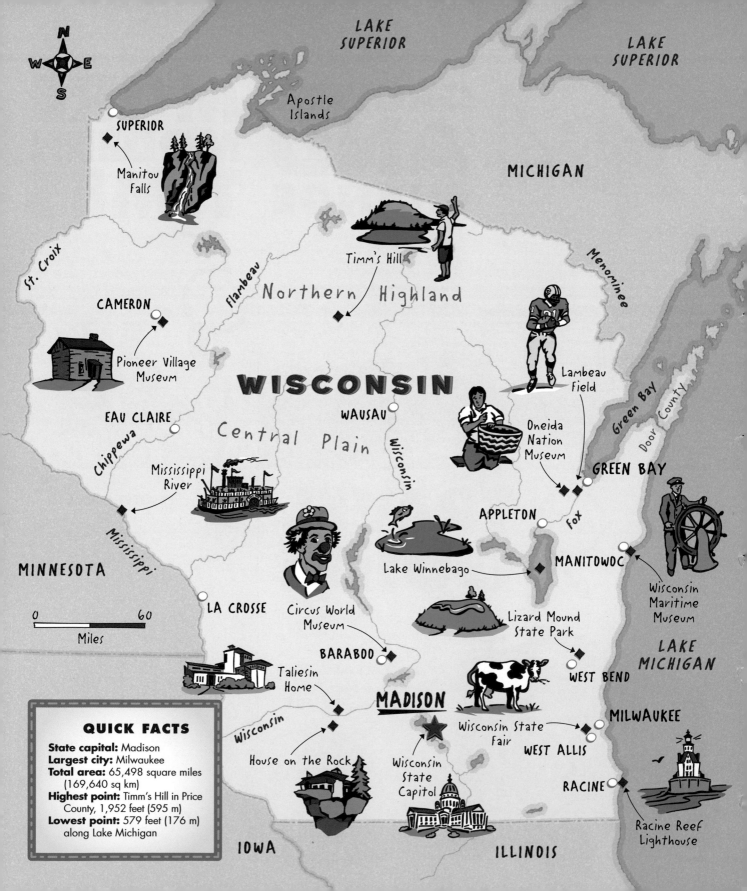

LAKE SUPERIOR

LAKE SUPERIOR

N W E S

MICHIGAN

Apostle Islands

SUPERIOR

Manitou Falls

St. Croix

Flambeau

Northern Highland

Timm's Hill

CAMERON

Pioneer Village Museum

Menominee

EAU CLAIRE

Chippewa

WISCONSIN

Central Plain

WAUSAU

Wisconsin

Lambeau Field

Oneida Nation Museum

Green Bay

Door County

GREEN BAY

Mississippi River

APPLETON

Fox

MINNESOTA

Mississippi

MANITOWOC

Wisconsin Maritime Museum

LAKE MICHIGAN

0 60 Miles

LA CROSSE

Circus World Museum

Lake Winnebago

BARABOO

Lizard Mound State Park

WEST BEND

Taliesin Home

MADISON

Wisconsin State Fair

MILWAUKEE

Wisconsin

House on the Rock

Wisconsin State Capitol

WEST ALLIS

RACINE

Racine Reef Lighthouse

IOWA

ILLINOIS

QUICK FACTS

State capital: Madison
Largest city: Milwaukee
Total area: 65,498 square miles (169,640 sq km)
Highest point: Timm's Hill in Price County, 1,952 feet (595 m)
Lowest point: 579 feet (176 m) along Lake Michigan

CANADA

Welcome to Wisconsin!

HOW DID WISCONSIN GET ITS NAME?

Wisconsin's Algonquian-speaking Native Americans lived near a river they called Meskousing, "the river that meanders through a red place." The "red place" probably refers to the reddish stone of the bluffs found at the Wisconsin Dells. In 1673, French explorer Louis Jolliet, accompanied on his journey by Native Americans, called it Miskonsing on a map. Louis Hennepin, a French priest and explorer, called the same river Misconsin, which he thought meant "strong current." The French changed that name to Ouisconsin, and eventually the U.S. Congress made it Wisconsin.

WISCONSIN

LAKE HURON

CANADA

MICHIGAN

LAKE ERIE

8

READ ABOUT

A rocky outcrop
over Devil's Lake
State Park, near
Baraboo

CHAPTER ONE

LAND

★

THOUSANDS OF LAKES, CRAGGY BLUFFS WHERE EAGLES NEST, UNEXPECTED DIPS AND HILLS, AND TOWERING ROCK FORMATIONS MARK THE WISCONSIN LANDSCAPE. In the state's 65,498 square miles (169,640 square kilometers), you'll also find rounded hills and valleys that seem untouched by time, along with some of the most fertile soil in the world. The state is relatively flat. Its highest point is Timm's Hill at just 1,952 feet (595 meters). And its lowest point is 579 feet (176 m) along Lake Michigan.

A kayaker on Lake Superior explores the sea caves on Devil's Island. Lake Superior is a remnant from the great Wisconsin glaciation of the last ice age.

WORD TO KNOW

glaciers *slow-moving bodies of ice*

THE ICE AGE

Until about 12,000 years ago, **glaciers** spread outward from the Arctic, covering most of Canada and the northern United States. This period of ice is called the Wisconsin glaciation, because its effects are most clearly seen in this state. As the ice melted, it left cone-shaped hollows filled with water, ridges formed by small particles of rock, and long, narrow hills. The glaciers deposited huge rocks and sand, trapping some of the ice. When this ice melted, it made an immense lake called Glacial Lake Wisconsin. Water flowed out and created channels in which the Wisconsin and other rivers still flow. The water that was trapped in the lowest land became Devil's Lake. Glaciers retreating into Canada gouged out three Great Lakes: Superior, Michigan, and Huron.

Ice did not cover all of Wisconsin. The southwestern part of the state is a region of flat-topped hills and steep-sided valleys called the Driftless Area. *Drift* is a term for the rocky debris a glacier leaves behind.

LAND REGIONS

Four primary land regions make up the state of Wisconsin. Geologists call them Western Upland, Northern Highland, Eastern Ridges and Lowlands, and Central Plain.

Western Upland

The Western Upland has high hills and spectacular valleys. It has good soil, but the hills are usually too steep to farm easily.

Northern Highland

This area in the far north was once high mountains, but they were worn away millions of years ago. Still, the highest point in the state is located here. This region has poor soil for agriculture, but vast forests known as the Northwoods thrive. Lakes and swamps, dug out by the glaciers, dot the forests. Northern Wisconsin includes part of the Gogebic Iron Range, which was mined for 80 years until all the iron was gone, around 1965.

Wisconsin Geo-Facts

Along with the state's geographical highlights, this chart ranks Wisconsin's land, water, and total area compared to all other states.

Total area; rank . . . . . . 65,498 square miles (169,640 sq km); 23rd
    Land; rank . . . . 54,310 square miles (140,663 sq km); 25th
    Water; rank . . . . 11,188 square miles (28,977 sq km); 4th
    Inland water; rank . . . 1,830 square miles (4,740 sq km); 11th
    Great Lakes; rank . . . . 9,358 square miles (24,237 sq km); 2nd
Geographic center . . . . Wood County,
9 miles (14.5 km) southeast of Marshfield
Latitude . . . . 42° 30′ N to 47° 3′ N
Longitude . . . . 86° 49′ W to 92° 54′ W
Highest point . . . . Timm's Hill in Price County, 1,952 feet (595 m)
Lowest point . . . . 579 feet (176 m) along Lake Michigan
Largest city . . . . Milwaukee

Source: U.S. Census Bureau, 2010 census

Wisconsin ranks in the middle of all states when it comes to land area, but because it borders two Great Lakes, it ranks fourth in amount of shoreline.

Wisconsin's rich, fertile soil makes it the perfect place for farms, such as these in Dodge County.

WORDS TO KNOW

erosion *the process of land being worn away by wind, water, or other factors*

irrigation *watering land by artificial means to promote plant growth*

Eastern Ridges and Lowlands

These ridges are several miles wide and have sharp drops on one side and gentle slopes on the other. Between these ridges are plains, where good soil has accumulated. Today, the plains are covered with farms.

Central Plain

This region consists of flat areas, low hills, and startling rocks that rise out of the landscape, especially near Camp Douglas. These are hard rocks that survived the **erosion** of the land around them. Several areas within the Central Plain have a few trees. The soil of this region is sandy and not good for agriculture without regular **irrigation**.

Wisconsin Topography

Use the color-coded elevation chart to see on the map Wisconsin's high points (orange) and low points (green to dark green). Elevation is measured as the distance above or below sea level.

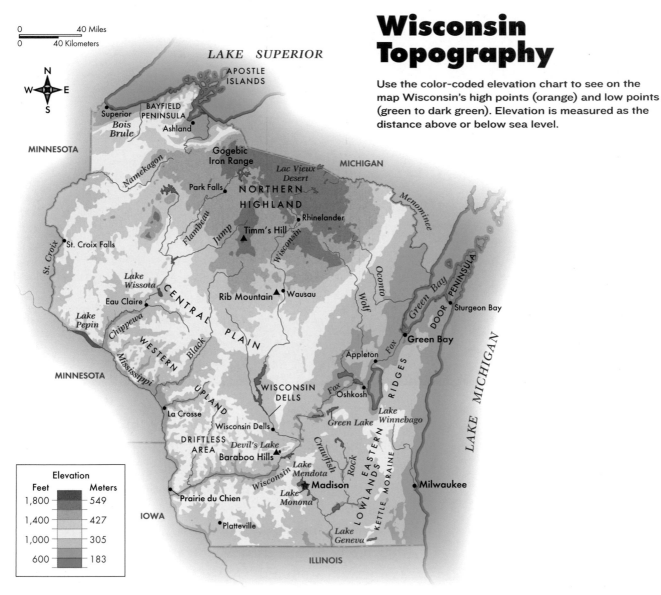

Elevation

Feet		Meters
1,800		549
1,400		427
1,000		305
600		183

LAND O' LAKES

The Ojibwe people in Wisconsin call Lake Superior Gichigami, or "big water." Lake Superior covers more surface area than any other lake in the world. It forms part of Wisconsin's northern border. Today, Lake Superior is connected to the Atlantic Ocean by a series of canals and rivers that together are called the St. Lawrence Seaway.

You can see some of the oldest geological formations in Wisconsin at Rib Mountain near Wausau. The huge chunk of quartzite rock that makes up the 1,924-foot (586 m) mountain is more than a billion years old.

Raspberry Island is one of 22 islands that are part of the Apostle Island chain in Lake Superior.

Door County has more miles of shoreline—250 miles (400 km)—more lighthouses (10), and more state parks (5) than any other county in the United States.

In Lake Superior, off Bayfield Peninsula, are the 22 Apostle Islands. Twenty-one of them (excluding populated Madeline Island) and 12 miles (19 km) of mainland shoreline make up the Apostle Islands National Lakeshore.

Door County is a peninsula in eastern Wisconsin that projects into Lake Michigan to form Green Bay. The waters around the top of the peninsula are treacherous, which caused the French to call the area *port des morts*, meaning "death's door." Just off the tip of the peninsula is Washington Island.

Vacationers have been drawn to the more than 15,000 lakes tucked away in the woods of northern Wisconsin since the 19th century, when railroads made getting to them easy. The 3,200 lakes in the area around Minocqua are a major tourist destination. Vilas County has the most lakes in the state—1,318 of them. Some lakes have never been named, and 116 lakes in the state are called Mud Lake.

Wisconsin's largest lake is Winnebago, covering 137,708 acres (55,772 hectares). Winnebago is shallow, with an average depth of only 15.5 feet (4.7 m). At the opposite extreme, Wisconsin's deepest natural lake is Green Lake in Green Lake County. It has a maximum depth of 236 feet (72 m).

Lac Vieux Desert is a lake on the Wisconsin-Michigan border. French explorers named it after a deserted Indian planting ground on one of its islands. The Wisconsin River flows out of its southwestern corner.

THE MISSISSIPPI AND OTHER RIVERS

The Mississippi River forms the southwestern boundary of Wisconsin. The Mississippi is one of America's most important rivers, running from Lake Itasca in Minnesota to the Gulf of Mexico. The rapidly flowing Chippewa River deposits sand and other debris into the Mississippi, causing a natural dam above the mouth of the Chippewa. That dam forms Lake Pepin, a wide spot in the Mississippi River that stretches from Bay City to the town of Pepin.

The Wisconsin River is another important waterway. It runs from Lac Vieux Desert in Vilas County in the far north to the Mississippi River in the southwest. It is 430 miles (692 km) long. The Wisconsin Dells is a region of the southern Wisconsin River where the wide, flat river narrows and flows through high cliffs and around red sandstone formations.

Northern Wisconsin has many waterfalls, especially on the Black and Brule rivers. The highest, as tall as a 16-story skyscraper, is Big Manitou Falls on the Black River in Pattison State Park. A ridge of resistant volcanic

The Wisconsin Dells is an area on the Wisconsin River noted for its sandstone rock formations.

rock between 10 and 20 miles (16 and 32 km) inland from Lake Superior forms many waterfalls, including those in Amnicon Falls State Park on the Amnicon River.

Winding along part of Wisconsin's border with Minnesota, the St. Croix River is part of the National Wild and Scenic Rivers System. Wisconsin's Wolf River is also a Wild and Scenic River, the only one wholly within Wisconsin.

Dams have created or enlarged many lakes, including Lake Wissota and Chippewa **Flowage**. Water that collected behind the Chippewa River's Winter Dam formed the Chippewa Flowage. The vast flowage swallowed up 10 smaller lakes and important Native American territory.

CLIMATE

Most of Wisconsin is cold and snowy in the winter and hot and humid in the summer, though near the Great Lakes it's cooler in summer and just a bit warmer in winter. Broad weather patterns sweeping across the continent affect Wisconsin. The climate pattern is called temperate continental. The entire state usually gets enough snow for winter sports, especially in the north. The most snow often falls along the shore of Lake Superior.

Wisconsin has experienced several devastating tornadoes and storms. In 2011, a type of severe thunderstorm called a blowdown, or straight-line wind, struck northwestern Wisconsin. The wind gusts exceeded 60 miles per hour (97 kph), with smaller pockets of winds blowing more than 100 miles per hour (160 kph). The blowdowns destroyed large tracts of forestland.

Weather Report

This chart shows record temperatures (high and low) for the state, as well as average temperatures (January and July) and average annual precipitation.

Record high temperature . . . . 114°F (46°C)
at Wisconsin Dells on July 13, 1936
Record low temperature . . . . –55°F (–48°C)
at Couderay on February 4, 1996
Average January temperature, Milwaukee . . . . 22°F (–6°C)
Average July temperature, Milwaukee . . . . 72°F (22°C)
Average yearly precipitation, Milwaukee . . . 34.8 inches (88.4 cm)

Source: National Climatic Data Center, NESDIS, NOAA, U.S. Department of Commerce

PLANT LIFE

A huge forest once stretched from New England to the Mississippi River, covering the northern half of Wisconsin. Pines were abundant, as were hardwoods such as maple, birch, ironwood, and fir. In the 19th century, lumber companies cut down most of these trees. But around 1911, Wisconsin created a tree nursery to grow millions of replacement trees. Wisconsin's 1.5- million-acre (600,000 ha) national forest was created in 1933 to preserve what was left of the Northwoods after most of the old trees had been cut.

Hickory, beech, ash, oak, hemlock, and elm are some of the hardwood **deciduous** trees that grow along the southern edge of the Northwoods and throughout the southern half of the state.

Wisconsin's abundant forests, however, are often the victims of the forces of nature. The emerald ash borer is a green beetle that destroys ash trees. Originally from Asia, this invasive species bores holes in trees. This blocks the flow of nutrients as they rise up the tree's trunk from its roots to its branches.

Wisconsin has a great variety of plant life besides trees. Wild cranberries thrive in its marshes and

Since 1911, more than 1.5 billion tree seedlings have been grown in Wisconsin state nurseries.

WORD TO KNOW

deciduous *types of trees that lose their leaves each year*

Wisconsin National Park Areas

This map shows some of Wisconsin's national parks, monuments, preserves, and other areas protected by the National Park Service.

LAKE SUPERIOR

Apostle Islands NL

Superior

Ashland

MINNESOTA

North Country NST

MICHIGAN

Park Falls

St. Croix NSR

Rhinelander

Menominee

St. Croix Falls

St. Croix

Flambeau

Wausau

Wisconsin

Eau Claire

Ice Age NST

Green Bay

Sturgeon Bay

Chippewa

Appleton

Fox

Green Bay

Mississippi

MINNESOTA

Oshkosh

LAKE MICHIGAN

N
W   E
S

La Crosse

Lake Winnebago

0   40 Miles
0   40 Kilometers

Wisconsin Dells

Ice Age NST

Wisconsin

Madison

Milwaukee

National Park area

NL   National Lakeshore
NSR   National Scenic River
NST   National Scenic Trail

Prairie du Chien

IOWA

ILLINOIS

GAYLORD NELSON: FOUNDER OF EARTH DAY

Wisconsin senator Gaylord Nelson (1916–2005), a native of Clear Lake in Polk County, cared about the environment. Nelson had the idea of establishing Earth Day as an annual day to pay attention to the planet. The first Earth Day was held in 1970. In 1995, President Clinton presented Nelson with the Presidential Medal of Freedom, the highest honor given to U.S. civilians. Today, people celebrate Earth Day every April 22 by planting trees, conserving gasoline, and encouraging other planet-friendly activities.

? **Want to know more?** Visit www.factsfornow.scholastic.com and enter the keyword **Wisconsin**.

Pickerelweed

swamps. A marsh called Crex Meadows near Grantsburg is a vast spread of wire grass, once used to make carpets. In addition to wild rice, which has long been an important food for Native Americans, lotus, pickerelweed, duckweed, arrowhead, and cattails grow in the marshes. Many ducks breed among the marsh plants, and northern pike lay their eggs in marshes.

ANIMAL LIFE

Northern pike venture out from marshes into the lakes of northern Wisconsin. These speckled fish often reach 3 or 4 feet (0.9 or 1.2 m) in length. Much scarcer is the smaller muskellunge, which gets its name from an Ojibwe word meaning "ugly pike."

Lake Winnebago is home to the world's largest population of sturgeon. These fish produce eggs, called caviar, which people consider a delicacy. Wisconsin has excellent trout and walleye fishing. Other smaller fish found in most lakes include rock bass, yellow perch, crappies, bluegills, and sunfish. More than 300 species of snails, oysters, mussels, and other **mollusks** also live there.

WORD TO KNOW

mollusks *shellfish*

ALIEN INVADER: RUSSIAN ZEBRA MUSSELS

The Russian zebra mussel has made its way from the Great Lakes into many small lakes and rivers. The mussels clog water-intake systems and boat engines, and they pose a serious challenge to native species if not kept under control.

THE WOLF DEBATE

Wolves have existed in Wisconsin for about 10,000 years. By 1975, wolves were considered an endangered species, after nearly being hunted to extinction. At that time, Wisconsin's wolf packs resettled along the Minnesota border. To aid the wolf population, the state began a program to reintroduce them into Wisconsin by legally protecting wolves and their habitats from hunters. By the 1990s, Wisconsin's wolf population was growing rapidly.

Environmentalists and animal-rights activists were pleased that wolves were once again thriving in their native territories. But when Wisconsin began to allow legal wolf hunting in 2012, controversy erupted. Wolf activists claim it is cruel and inhumane to hunt wolves, especially after surviving near-extinction. Supporters of legal hunting say that the wolf population needs to be kept at low levels. This would protect other wildlife, including animals that live on ranches, as well as the wolves themselves.

With 408 different species of birds that live in or migrate through the state, Wisconsin is a bird-watcher's paradise. Large birds such as eagles, hawks, pheasants, and wild turkeys are common throughout the state.

One of the most beloved sounds of the northern lakes is the loon's call, a haunting, yodel-like noise that echoes over the lakes at dusk in summer. But these black and white relatives of ducks can be hard to find because one migrating pair will usually claim an entire lake as its home.

One million Canada geese visit Horicon National Wildlife Refuge near Waupun each year. They are attracted by the 32,000-acre (13,000 ha) Horicon Marsh, the largest cattail marsh in the United States. Some live there year-round, but about 300,000 migrating geese may be on the marsh waters at any one time in the fall, along with about 220 other species of birds.

The eastern part of the state, from Green Bay south, is home to most of Wisconsin's preserves and sanctuaries. Wild turkeys, once scarce, were reintroduced to Wisconsin in 1976. Now they thrive within Wisconsin's borders.

The first Europeans in Wisconsin hunted beavers, muskrats, foxes, coyotes, and bears for their fur. All of these mammals can still be found in the state. Wild bison, or American buffalo, have been gone since about 1830, but the animals are bred on several farms. Elk and moose were hunted to near-extinction, but recent reintroduction efforts have resulted in a slow but steady increase in their numbers. Elk had completely disappeared from the state for more than 100 years, until

Whooping cranes

Many black bears make their home in Wisconsin. This one scratches up against a birch tree while a cub watches.

1995. Wisconsin's Department of Natural Resources oversees the state's reintroduction programs.

The most common large mammal in the state is the white-tailed deer. These deer thrive on the food they forage on the state's farms and occasionally in people's gardens. In some areas, there may be as many as 100 deer per square mile (40 per sq km). Black bears are less common, but they are still plentiful.

PROTECTING THE ENVIRONMENT

Many Wisconsinites work to make their state a healthy home for plants, animals, and humans. Waste from factories has often ended up in lakes and rivers, polluting the state's waters. The Wisconsin legislature has passed laws to prevent factories from dumping waste, and factories are working to make their operations cleaner. The state also has created programs to help preserve farmland and natural areas. The Wisconsin Department of Natural Resources aims to promote clean and healthy environments for people and wildlife.

ENDANGERED SPECIES

Wisconsin has a smaller list of endangered animals than many other states. It includes the Karner blue butterfly, the piping plover, and the Canada lynx.

Karner blue butterfly

READ ABOUT

The Ojibwe used picture writing, such as these symbols, to tell stories.

10,000 BCE
People first enter what is now Wisconsin

4000 BCE
Burial mounds are built at what is now Copper Culture State Park

▲ **50–100 CE**
The Woodland Indians settle in the region

CHAPTER TWO

FIRST PEOPLE

★

MORE THAN 12,000 YEARS AGO, AS THE LAST ICE AGE WAS RETREATING, EARLY HUMANS WANDERED INTO WISCONSIN. They probably moved in family groups. Using spears and great skill, they hunted woolly mammoths and mastodons. When these huge animals disappeared, the early people who depended on them moved on.

▲ 1000–1300
A community of Mound Builders thrives near the Crawfish River

1500
The Anishinabi settle along the Great Lakes

1600
Some 20,000 Native Americans live in the region

Thirteen-year-old Donald Baldwin was digging in the dirt of Oconto County in 1952, when he found a 6,000-year-old burial mound containing skeletons and copper tools. The area is now Copper Culture State Park.

EARLY METALWORK

The first people in the region (called Paleo-Indians by **archaeologists**) found copper near Lake Superior. They broke the metal free from rocks and pounded it into spears, knives, and jewelry. Tools made from Wisconsin copper have been found throughout the country, suggesting that the Paleo-Indians also traded the metal.

THE WOODLAND INDIANS

Many Native people moved through Wisconsin, primarily to hunt. By about 2,000 years ago, some began to settle to raise crops and build villages. Their main crops were corn, squash, and beans, which later Indian peoples called the "Three Sisters." The Woodland peoples made pottery in which to store their harvests. They created bows and arrows, as well as canoes made of birch bark. They also made containers, called *mocucks*, from birch bark. These people harvested the soft bark of birch trees in the spring when it was strong and pliable. Then they steamed the damp bark over fire. As it cooled, it held whatever shape it was put in.

The Woodland people participated in special ceremonies and traditions. They smoked tobacco or red willow bark to communicate with the spirits that played a role in their rituals. During the Woodland period, Native Americans of the Midwest

The Woodland people made containers called mocucks from birch bark.

Building an effigy mound

WORD TO KNOW

effigy *a figure of a person or animal*

built mounds in the shape of animals, sometimes 200 feet (60 m) long. Called **effigy** mounds, some were used for burials. Mounds that look like bears, birds, and turtles are among those that have been found. Few are left today, but Lizard Mound State Park at West Bend features 31 effigy mounds. The most prominent is a huge lizard.

The lives of the Woodland peoples, even of different groups, were similar. Food was everyone's main concern. The people hunted, fished, planted, and harvested. To build canoes that could be carried overland, they cut down birch trees with stone or metal tools. They stretched the birch bark over cedar ribs. When the Indians didn't need to carry their boats, they made heavier ones out of hollowed-out logs.

SEE IT HERE!

THE MYSTERY OF AZTALAN

Three big earthen platforms near the Crawfish River in Jefferson County left 19th-century fur traders bewildered. What were these flat-topped pyramids, and who made them? In 1850, a scientist who investigated the site urged that it be preserved, but farmers ignored him and plowed it for crops for many years. By 1922, only a few of the more than 40 original mounds remained. A group of concerned citizens bought these last mounds and in 1927 gave the property to the Wisconsin Archaeological Society. Archaeologists discovered that the mounds had been part of an entire village surrounded by a stockade fence of tall posts. Villagers had thrived there between 1000 and 1300. They hunted, fished, and farmed on the floodplain of the Crawfish River. Archaeologists believe that the mounds partly served the village's religious purposes.

No one knows why the city was abandoned. Archaeologists have reconstructed the stockade and two mounds, which you can now see in Aztalan State Park.

Native American Peoples

(Before European Contact)

This map shows the general area of Native American peoples before European settlers arrived.

In addition to working with birch bark to create buckets, women wove mats for floor coverings out of bulrushes and cattails. They made baskets out of sweetgrass or willow stems. They tanned, or softened, deer hide for clothing by soaking it in water that contained such things as deer organs. Chemicals in these animal parts broke down the tough material, softening the hide. Finished clothing was decorated with porcupine quills dyed with colored plants.

THE MENOMINEE

It's not possible to say for certain that any group originated in Wisconsin—except for the Menominee. Only these people have an origin story that says they began right where they are today, in Wisconsin.

The Menominee originated in what is now Wisconsin.

They tell of a great Bear that emerged from the ground near Green Bay. Great Spirit let Bear change into the first Menominee man. Bear-man called down Bald Eagle, who turned into Eagle-man. Together, these two collected other animals that Great Spirit turned into other Menominees.

Menominee is an abbreviated form of the full name Omaeqnominniwuk, which means "people of the wild rice."

KEEPERS OF THE FAITH

The Anishinabi lived near the mouth of the St. Lawrence River on the East Coast, until the Iroquois forced them out. According to legend, a magical shell showed them the direction to move. Great Spirit told the Anishinabi to find the "food that grows on water."

Picture Yourself . . .

Preparing to Become an Ojibwe Shaman

As you've grown, you've been studying the world around you. Perhaps you've shown a special interest in plants and how they can be used as medicines. The elders have asked you to become a **shaman**. You go on a vision quest—a period of fasting and prayer that causes you to experience visions. You identify your personal guardian spirits, who tell you that you will become a shaman.

You study birch-bark scrolls on which are painted the wisdom of the Ojibwe people. Day by day, you learn which plants are useful for making medicines that heal illnesses and wounds. You are taught sacred prayers, dances, and songs that invoke the power to heal in those plants.

Now you are ready to be initiated. In the ceremony, you symbolically die and are brought back to life as a new spiritual leader of your people.

WORD TO KNOW

shaman *a priest who cures people and communicates with the spirit world for the group*

In the upper Great Lakes region, they found wild rice growing in the rivers and lakes, and by 1500 they decided to settle. They gradually occupied most of northern Wisconsin.

Great Spirit divided the Anishinabi into three groups. It made the Ojibwe (also spelled Ojibway and Ojibwa) "keepers of the faith" and the Potawatomi "keepers of the sacred fire." The Odawa (also called the Ottawa) were made "trader people."

Ojibwe is also spelled "Chippewa," which is simply a different pronunciation of "Ojibwe." In

An Ojibwe medicine man and his family standing near their birch wigwam

recent years, some have returned to the name Anishinabi (plural: Anishinabek), which translates to "original people." But their reservation names still include Ojibwe (or Chippewa).

THE HO-CHUNK, OR WINNEBAGO

The Ho-chunk, or "people of the big voice," lived near Green Bay. They spoke a Siouan language. For several hundred years, others called them Winnebagos. A neighboring Algonquin community gave them the name, which probably means "stinky people." In 1993, the U.S. government allowed them to use Ho-chunk as their official name. The Ho-chunk say that Earthmaker (Manuna) created four brothers and sent them down to Earth at Green Bay. They carried with them tobacco and fire. Many Ho-chunks believe they were the mound builders of southern Wisconsin, though there is no evidence to support this.

Betsy Thunder, a Ho-Chunk medicine woman, of Black River Falls

Also speaking a Siouan language were the Dakota, who lived primarily in Minnesota and had only a few villages on the eastern side of the Mississippi. Farther south lived another Siouan group, the Ioway people, who mainly dwelled across the river in Iowa. Both of these groups later moved westward. The Ojibwe probably drove the Dakota out of northern Wisconsin, but once the Dakota had horses, they also left because they wanted to hunt buffalo. By 1600, shortly before the arrival of Europeans in the region, some 20,000 Native Americans lived in what we now know as Wisconsin.

30

READ ABOUT

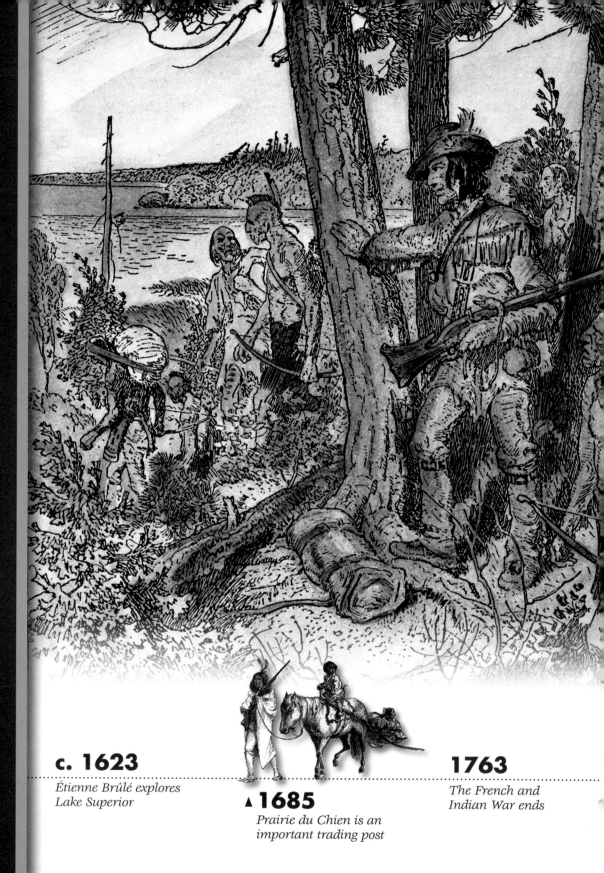

Between 1610 and 1624, Étienne Brûlé explored the area of the Great Lakes. He was the first European to see and describe Lakes Ontario, Erie, Superior, and Huron.

c. 1623

Étienne Brûlé explores Lake Superior

▲**1685**

Prairie du Chien is an important trading post

1763

The French and Indian War ends

CHAPTER THREE

EXPLORATION AND SETTLEMENT

★

IMAGINE BEING THE FIRST PERSON TO VENTURE OUT OF A COMMUNITY OF EUROPEANS LIVING IN THE WILDERNESS OF CENTRAL NEW FRANCE (CANADA). You set off with a few Indian guides, not knowing what you'll find or even if you'll return. That's what Étienne Brûlé did in about 1623. Nothing is known about his trip around Lake Superior, except that he didn't survive. What happened to him? We may never know.

1820s
Many Oneida move to Wisconsin

▲**1825**
The Erie Canal is opened

▲**1832**
The Black Hawk War takes place

French explorer Jean Nicolet arrived on the shores of Wisconsin, in 1634.

EARLY EUROPEANS

Eleven years after Brûlé set out, the governor of New France sent Jean Nicolet, a Frenchman who spoke Algonquian languages, to explore the region past the Straits of Mackinac, where lakes Superior, Huron, and Michigan come together.

Nicolet hoped to find a route to China and introduce Christianity to its people. He and his men probably paddled their canoes down the northern shore of Lake Michigan into Green Bay. Believing he had reached China, he donned an outfit that he assumed was Asian and stepped out to greet the Potawatomi people he found there. He stayed long enough to make arrangements to trade for furs and establish La Baye, the first trading post in Wisconsin. The Potawatomi were not yet residents of Wisconsin—they were probably just visiting from Michigan.

In 1661, two other fur traders, Pierre Radisson and Médard Groseilliers, and a Catholic priest, Father René Ménard, followed Nicolet. They explored the shores of

Lake Superior and then paddled into Lake Michigan and up the Fox River. They carried their canoes to the Wisconsin River and then went on to the Mississippi.

In 1665, Father Claude Allouez, a Roman Catholic priest, arrived in Wisconsin and established a mission on Lake Superior. He said Catholic Mass for the Native Americans, marking the first time this religious service was held in the Midwest. In 1669, he returned to establish a mission at La Baye, which became Green Bay. Father Jacques Marquette and Louis Jolliet departed from this mission to explore the Mississippi River in 1673.

TRAPPERS, TRADERS, AND EMPIRES

Frenchmen called voyageurs engaged in the fur trade, traveling the rivers, carrying furs and other goods, and trading with Native Americans. Voyageurs introduced guns to the Indians. In the course of the voyageurs' work, they learned more about Indian lands than any other foreigners of the day. Many married Indian women.

Different Native American groups and European empires claimed Wisconsin and its rich natural resources. The French king claimed all of Canada, which included Wisconsin at that time. But the British won both Canada and the Old Northwest. This area included Wisconsin, as a result of the French and Indian War, which ended in 1763. The Old Northwest took in the entire Great Lakes region, from Pennsylvania west to the Mississippi River and north of the Ohio River to Canada. It was a chunk of land bigger than the original 13 colonies.

When the American Revolution ended in 1783, Great Britain gave the region to the new United States. Britain kept Canada. Congress turned the Old Northwest into the Northwest Territory, splitting it up into smaller territories that were opened for settlement. Eventually, the

European Exploration of Wisconsin

The colored arrows on this map show the routes taken by explorers between 1634 and 1679.

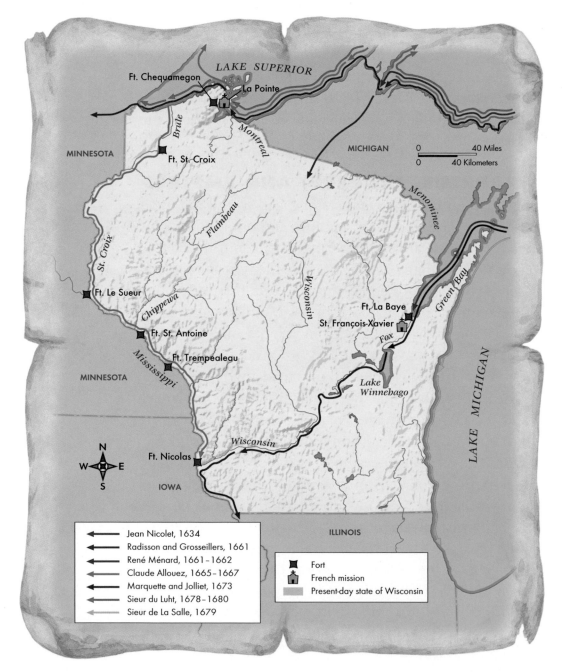

LAKE SUPERIOR

Ft. Chequamegon
La Pointe

MINNESOTA

Brule

Montreal

MICHIGAN

0   40 Miles
0   40 Kilometers

Ft. St. Croix

Flambeau

Menominee

St. Croix

Wisconsin

Ft. Le Sueur

Chippewa

Ft. La Baye
St. François-Xavier

Green Bay

Ft. St. Antoine

Ft. Trempealeau

Fox

Mississippi

MINNESOTA

Lake
Winnebago

LAKE MICHIGAN

Wisconsin

Ft. Nicolas

N
W   E
S

IOWA

ILLINOIS

◄── Jean Nicolet, 1634
◄── Radisson and Grosseillers, 1661
◄── René Ménard, 1661–1662
◄── Claude Allouez, 1665–1667
◄── Marquette and Jolliet, 1673
◄── Sieur du Luht, 1678–1680
◄── Sieur de La Salle, 1679

■ Fort
⌂ French mission
▨ Present-day state of Wisconsin

Northwest Territory became five and a half states: Ohio, Indiana, Illinois, Michigan, Wisconsin, and part of Minnesota.

MORE NATIVE PEOPLES

As European explorers, trappers, and traders began to enter Wisconsin, so did new Indian groups. The Iroquois Wars, or the Beaver Wars, had started in about 1670. The Iroquois, based in the New York area, forced other groups west. The Mesquaki, or Fox, entered Wisconsin from the north and gradually made their way south. They settled in southwestern Wisconsin and northern Illinois, and allied themselves with another Algonquian-speaking group called the Sac, or Sauk. Together, these groups are known today as the Sac and Fox.

Lead had not been important to the Native people until the French began trading guns for furs. Then they learned that it was useful in making lead shot. The Ho-chunk and Mesquaki started mining for lead when firearms arrived in their area. One village the Native Americans founded near the lead mines later became Prairie du Chien, French for "Prairie of the Dog," named after an early Mesquaki chief who lived on the prairie. In springtime, fur traders and Native Americans met on the prai-

MINI-BIO

CHARLES DE LANGLADE: WISCONSIN'S FIRST EUROPEAN SETTLER

Before his death, Charles de Langlade (1729–1800) claimed to have fought in 99 battles. Langlade was a French fur trader, Indian warrior, and the first European settler of Wisconsin. He was born in Michigan to a French father and Odawa Indian mother. He began fighting in battles as a boy, and in 1748, he led Indian forces for the French in trying to oust British traders from the Ohio Valley. In 1755, Langlade helped defeat the British at Fort Duquesne (now Pittsburgh, Pennsylvania). After the French lost the French and Indian War, he offered his talents to the British. He moved his family to Green Bay, becoming the state's first part-white settler. Sometimes called the father of Wisconsin, he was known to the Indians as A-ke-wau-ge-ke-tau-so, which means "He who is fierce for the land."

? Want to know more? Visit www.factsfornow.scholastic.com and enter the keyword **Wisconsin**.

Many trappers and their families traveled to Prairie du Chien, a trading post.

rie to trade. Prairie du Chien was neutral ground. Rival groups put down their weapons before meeting there. By 1685, it was an important trading post.

French explorers learned of Wisconsin's lead deposits from Indians. Not long after that, trader Nicolas Perrot located the Indians' lead mines. When the French seriously considered wiping out the Mesquaki to take their mines, Perrot stopped them.

The Mesquaki and Sauk were frequently at war, especially with the Ojibwe and then the French. The French wanted the right to use the rivers in Mesquaki lands, but the Indians objected, especially after the French decided they wanted the lead mines the Indians had been working.

The Native American way of life changed drastically in the 17th century. Indians had adjusted to firearms and European trade. However, many died from

European diseases or were enslaved by white men. Native Americans responded in different ways. Some fought with European weapons. Others migrated to areas free from whites. Still others joined forces with other Indian groups or surrendered to European power.

The Potawatomi of Michigan, also called Neshnabek, a variation of Anishinabe, settled near Green Bay. They moved south from there and soon occupied an area that included southern Wisconsin and Michigan, northern Illinois and Indiana, and part of Ohio.

Their villages were collections of wicki-ups, which were domed houses made of bent **saplings** covered with bark. The Potawatomi grew crops in summer and hunted in winter. In spring, they collected the sap of the sugar maples to make sugar and syrup.

Many Potawatomi allied themselves with the French in Wisconsin. They sent war parties to fight the Mesquaki and took over their land in southwestern Wisconsin. During the French and Indian War, they even sent parties far to the east to fight the British. Later, when the British ousted the French from Wisconsin, most Potawatomi tried to avoid the British.

WORD TO KNOW

saplings *young trees*

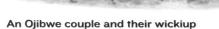

An Ojibwe couple and their wickiup

UNITED STATES CONTROL

Even though the British gave the Northwest Territory to the United States in 1783, British fur traders and soldiers stayed for another 30 years. During the War of 1812, the governor of Missouri Territory sent troops north to Prairie du Chien to build a fort. The British troops and their Native American allies forced the Americans to surrender. The British kept possession of Prairie du Chien until the treaty ending the war was settled, and the British finally left the Northwest Territory.

The United States had already begun making agreements, or treaties, with various Indian nations in Wisconsin, as they tried to gain control of the land for future settlers. The first treaty in Wisconsin was with the Mesquaki and Sauk people, in 1804. Many other treaties followed over the next 50 years. As you will soon read, one treaty with the Ojibwe people erupted in controversy in 1974.

JOINING FORCES

In 1820, Lewis Cass, the governor of Michigan Territory, headed an expedition into Wisconsin. Cass's party included geologist Henry R. Schoolcraft. Schoolcraft published a book about the trip that combined history, geography, and an exciting story. His book enticed people to come to Wisconsin. After the Erie Canal opened in 1825, it was easier to reach Wisconsin. Boats could travel from New York through the Great Lakes. White settlers especially wanted the lead mines of southwestern Wisconsin.

In 1827, the Ho-chunk leader at La Crosse, Red Bird, led a brief rebellion against the U.S. soldiers who were coming into Wisconsin. To be pardoned by the government, the Ho-chunk had to give up more land. Soon they were being moved west of the Mississippi, although many of the people came back to Wisconsin.

Like the Sauk and Mesquaki, the Stockbridge and Munsee people were originally two different groups, both from the East. The Stockbridge were Mahicans from Stockbridge, Massachusetts. The Munsee were part of the Delaware Confederacy (or Lenape) in what is now New Jersey. The two peoples joined forces for protection from the Mohawks and Iroquois. The Christian Brothertown

This illustration shows a fur trader's homestead built close to an Ojibwe village.

people, an Algonquian group from New England, also joined them. These groups, as well as some Oneida people from New York, came into Wisconsin in the 1820s and bought land from the Menominee. The first public schoolteacher in the state was a Stockbridge Mahican woman who opened a school in 1828 in Kaukauna.

In 1830, the Potawatomi were forced to cede, or give up, their lands—about 5 million acres (2 million ha)—to the United States. Eventually, they signed more treaties than any other group. The U.S. government repeatedly moved them across the Mississippi, each time to less desirable land.

The Mesquaki and Sauk people had sold some of their land in southwestern Wisconsin to the U.S. government, but they tried to keep their homeland where the Rock and Mississippi rivers meet in Illinois. Leading the fight was a man named Black Hawk. The rebellion he led came to be called the Black Hawk War.

In 1832, the Illinois governor called up a small army, including an officer named Abraham Lincoln, to chase Black Hawk and his warriors northward into Wisconsin. The army defeated the Native Americans in the Battle of Bad Axe. This was the last battle fought east of the Mississippi River between U.S. troops and Native Americans. Black Hawk surrendered at Prairie du Chien. The land that is now Wisconsin was about to change.

READ ABOUT

Peter Legacy, a
French Canadian
immigrant, with his
family in front of
their log cabin in
Washburn in 1895

1836

*Henry Dodge becomes
governor of Wisconsin
Territory*

1848

*Wisconsin becomes
a state*

1854

*The Ojibwe are
granted reservations
in Wisconsin*

CHAPTER FOUR

GROWTH AND CHANGE

★

I N THE 19TH CENTURY, SETTLERS WERE MORE LIKELY TO COME TO WISCONSIN FOR LEAD MINING THAN FOR FARMING OR THE FUR TRADE. By 1830, more than 4,000 miners worked in the lead mines of southwestern Wisconsin.

▲1865
Ezekiel Gillespie demands to vote

1871
Peshtigo suffers a devastating fire

▲1884
Mining in the Gogebic Iron Range begins

Many immigrants came to call Wisconsin home. Here, a Norwegian family gathers for a picnic celebration in a park in Larson City, around 1873.

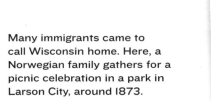

SEE IT HERE!

MAKING AMMUNITION

"Lead shot" is the word for tiny balls of lead that are loaded into a casing, or shell, to be fired from a shotgun. To make lead shot, workers dropped molten, or liquid, lead through holes in a copper plate from the top of a high tower. The small globs would round out as they fell down a shaft into cooling water. There's an old shot tower with a 120-foot-long (37 m) shaft at Tower Hill State Park near Spring Green.

IMMIGRANTS

Southern mine owners brought enslaved people with them. Then, during the 1830s, miners began to immigrate to Wisconsin from Cornwall, England, where the lead mines had run out of ore. Wisconsin was one of the richest lead mining areas in the world. Because these miners worked underground, they were nicknamed "badgers," and Wisconsin later came to be known as the Badger State. In the 19th century, Europeans were drawn to America by stories of cheap, fertile land in the Midwest. Probably the first European immigrant to settle permanently in Wisconsin was a Norwegian named Ole Nattestad, who settled in Rock County in 1838.

In the 1840s and 1850s, British settlers led an early wave of immigrants into Wisconsin. They bought land and loaned English factory workers money to move there and farm it. Some opened factories and workshops. These British immigrants were early settlers in Dane, Iowa, and Lafayette Counties.

Many settlers were Yankees from New England or other areas of the eastern United States. They were soon joined by large numbers of Germans, who eventually became the largest immigrant group in Wisconsin. People from the German states of Prussia, Saxony, and Bavaria came to this region.

Former slaves from the southern United States formed Pleasant Ridge in Grant County. In 1848, Charles and Isaac Shepard were freed by their owner, who gave them 40 acres (16 ha) of land. With other newly freed slaves, they built a school and a church. White parishioners also attended the church, making the area unique in Wisconsin.

MINI-BIO

LAURA INGALLS WILDER: PIONEER AND WRITER

Born near Pepin, Laura Ingalls Wilder (1867–1957) spent her early childhood in western Wisconsin. She remembered the sights, smells, fun, and fears of living in a little log house her father built in the "Big Woods." Her restless "Pa" later moved the family by covered wagon to Minnesota, Iowa, and finally to the Dakotas. In the Dakotas, Laura married Almanzo Wilder, with whom she also moved a number of times. Wilder was in her 60s when her daughter, Rose, persuaded her to write the stories of her childhood. They became beloved as the Little House series of books.

? **Want to know more?** Visit www.factsfornow.scholastic.com and enter the keyword **Wisconsin**.

STATEHOOD

Congress rearranged sections of the Northwest Territory as they gained enough settlers—60,000 were required—to make a state. At various times, today's Wisconsin was part of Indiana, Illinois, and Michigan. In 1836, Wisconsin was separated from Michigan and became a territory. The Wisconsin Territory included Minnesota, Iowa, and part of the Dakotas. Henry Dodge, who had fought fiercely against the Indians in the Black Hawk War, was named territorial governor.

By 1845, Wisconsin's population had reached 60,000 (the government didn't count Native Americans).

THE GATHERING OF MILWAUKEE

Three rivers gather at one site and run into Lake Michigan. They are the Milwaukee, the Menomonee (spelled differently from the Native American group), and the Kinnickinnic. Other people had lived at this site earlier, but the founding of a city there is credited to Canadian trader Solomon Juneau, who called it Juneautown, in about 1818. Other settlers arrived, and they used rocks and dirt to fill in swamps, enlarging the useful land.

Other traders settled nearby. Juneau's trading post soon became a town that had to compete with new communities started by Byron Kilbourn and George Walker. As the communities expanded toward each other, both Juneau and Kilbourn thought they each deserved to name the town. Their competition was so fierce that each built roads that wouldn't meet the roads the other built. In 1846, the territorial legislature combined the two communities, plus Walker's Point, under the name Milwaukee, from Potawatomi words meaning "gathering place." Even today, Milwaukee's bridges have to be built at an angle for the streets on the east side and the west side to meet.

With statehood in sight, Wisconsin residents drafted and approved a constitution. Wisconsin took its current boundaries when it became America's newest state on May 29, 1848.

THE FIGHT AGAINST SLAVERY

As Wisconsin became a state, forces were at work in the United States that would change the nation forever, and in bloody ways. People all over the country were at odds over the issue of slavery. Most Southern whites, and many Northerners, believed that enslaving people was necessary for the Southern economy. But other people believed that slavery was wrong.

As early as 1840, abolitionists (people who opposed slavery) formed a series of

A view of Milwaukee in 1853

Wisconsin: From Territory to Statehood

(1818–1848)

This map shows the original Wisconsin Territory and the area (outlined in red) that became the state of Wisconsin in 1848.

1818 Treaty Line

Lake of the Woods

Red

Lake Superior

British Possessions

Missouri

James

Wisconsin Territory, 1836–1838

Lake Michigan

Lake Huron

Lake Erie

MICHIGAN

Madison

Belmont

IOWA 1846

Unorganized Territory

Burlington

Illinois

Ohio

OHIO

MISSOURI

ILLINOIS

INDIANA

Mississippi

KENTUCKY

TENNESSEE

Legend:
- Northwest Territory
- Wisconsin Territory, 1836–1838
- Other territories
- Iowa Territory, 1838–1846
- States
- ★ Territorial capitals
- Wisconsin Territory, 1838–1848
- Iowa, 1846
- Wisconsin, 1848

N
W · E
S

FINALLY FREE

Joshua Glover escaped slavery and fled to Wisconsin in 1854 from his Missouri owner, B. S. Garland. Glover settled in Racine, a city on the Underground Railroad. When Garland learned of Glover's whereabouts, he went to court to demand his return. Two federal marshals accompanied him to Glover's home, where they brutally beat Glover before taking him to a Milwaukee jail.

Hundreds of antislavery Wisconsinites marched on the jail and set Glover free. Weeks of legal wrangling followed, especially after the sheriff of Racine County arrested Garland and the marshals. But by the time the legal issues were settled, Glover was in Canada and free.

WORD TO KNOW

fugitive *a person hiding from other people*

The capture of Joshua Glover, an escaped slave, by marshals in Racine

safe houses and hideouts that became known as the Underground Railroad to help slaves escape and move north to freedom. Americans who disagreed with slavery found it more difficult to help escaping slaves after Congress passed the **Fugitive** Slave Act in 1850. This act made it illegal to refuse to return a fugitive slave to his or her owner. But the Underground Railroad, and sometimes Native Americans, helped runaway slaves in Wisconsin.

Slaves traveling the Underground Railroad stopped at Janesville. From there, they went to Milton. Next, volunteers escorted the escapees across the state to Lake Michigan. There they could catch a boat to Canada.

NATIVE PEOPLE AND THEIR LAND

European settlers often forced Native Americans in southern Wisconsin to move. Sometimes Indians lost their land to white trickery. For example, the Lake Superior Ojibwe received a written promise that they could remain on their land if they did what the settlers told them to. The Ojibwe were ordered to go to Sandy Lake in Minnesota to get money they had been promised by the government. Three thousand people traveled 500 miles (800 km). On reaching Sandy Lake, they found neither the money nor food supplies. About 400 men, women, and children died while either waiting for supplies or walking home.

The Menominee were ordered to move to Minnesota. After Chief Oshkosh looked at the proposed reservation on the Crow Wing River, he said, "The poorest region in Wisconsin is better than the Crow Wing." He encouraged his people to stay where they were and ignore U.S. efforts to move them. The United States gave in and said the Menominee could stay in Wisconsin. The land they kept, though much smaller than their original lands, was at least within their original territory.

MINI-BIO

CHIEF BUFFALO: PRESERVER OF OJIBWE LAND

Angry and fearful that his people would be forced to give up their land, Chief Buffalo (1759?–1855) was determined to go to Washington, D.C., himself to talk to government leaders, even though he was more than 90 years old. He and another chief made the journey to meet with President Millard Fillmore. The chief told of government agents lying to his people again and again. The president agreed that it was wrong, and he canceled the order for the Ojibwe to move west. At a treaty meeting in 1854, the Ojibwe were granted six permanent reservations in northern Wisconsin. Chief Buffalo lived long enough to settle at Bad River.

? Want to know more? Visit www.factsfornow.scholastic.com and enter the keyword **Wisconsin**.

AN INFAMOUS DECISION

The 1787 Northwest Ordinance and the 1820 Missouri Compromise both made slavery illegal in the Wisconsin Territory. In the late 1830s and early 1840s, a Missouri slave named Dred Scott lived in Wisconsin with his owner, John Emerson. After Emerson died, Scott returned with Eliza Emerson to Missouri, where he sued her for his freedom. Scott's case was based on the time he spent in Wisconsin Territory and, before that, in the Free State of Illinois. Judges debated his case all the way to the Supreme Court, where, in 1857, his bid for freedom was rejected. Frederick Douglass, a leader of the antislavery movement, called it "an infamous decision." Still, Scott's efforts turned out to be heroic and historic. The Court's decision heated up the argument between pro-slavery and antislavery forces, which boiled over into Civil War between the North and the South in 1861. After the clash ended in 1865, the Constitution was amended to abolish slavery nationwide.

The Ho-chunk, too, managed to outlast government attempts to make them move, though they did not get a reservation. Instead, each family was allowed to keep 40 acres (16 ha) of land, scattered across 12 counties.

THE CIVIL WAR

A former New Yorker, Alvan Bovay, was angry that Congress had passed

In 1854, Alvan Bovay led a gathering at this schoolhouse in Ripon, which marked the beginning of the Republican Party.

the Kansas-Nebraska Act, which allowed slavery to expand farther west. At a meeting in Ripon, on March 20, 1854, Bovay and others suggested forming a new political party. This was the beginning of the Republican Party, which opposed the expansion of slavery. Word of the new and growing political party spread quickly. Its presidential candidate in the election of 1860 was Abraham Lincoln.

Pro-slavery Southern states withdrew, or seceded, from the United States after Lincoln won the election. Many immigrants did not believe the North should fight the South. Many others, though, were eager to help their new country. Hans Christian Heg, a Norwegian who had come to Wisconsin as a boy, formed a regiment of Norwegian soldiers. Colonel Heg was the highest-ranking Wisconsinite to die in combat. Back home in Wisconsin, women operated farms and took care of households while men were off fighting.

In 1865, the North finally won the long, bloody conflict. That same year, a black Milwaukeean, Ezekiel Gillespie, demanded the right to vote. When Wisconsin achieved statehood, the legislature had asked voters if African Americans should have the right to vote. Many voters left that question blank on the ballot. The state election board decided that a blank vote was a "no," and African Americans did not get to vote. Nearly two decades later, Gillespie took his case to the state supreme

Soon after the Civil War ended, Ezekiel Gillespie sued the state of Wisconsin for the right to vote.

OLD ABE

An Ojibwe found a pair of baby bald eaglets in 1861 and sold one to a white neighbor in Lac du Flambeau, who named it Old Abe in honor of the president. He gave Old Abe to the 8th Wisconsin Regiment at Eau Claire. Old Abe rode into 36 battles mounted on a perch. He lived in the capitol at Madison until he died in a fire in 1881.

court and won. Thanks in part to Gillespie's efforts,1,500 African Americans voted in state elections in 1866. Two years later, the Fourteenth Amendment to the U.S. Constitution gave all men over age 21 the right to vote.

EXPANDING INDUSTRY

After the war, immigrants began to come to America again—in huge numbers. They came as farmers or to work in booming Wisconsin industries. Southern Wisconsin had been a major grower of wheat until it became more profitable in the 19th century to grow wheat farther west. After the introduction of dairy cows in 1838, Wisconsin farmers turned their land into dairy farms. In 1864, the first cheese factory was opened in Ladoga, near Fond du Lac.

To process the wheat, flour mills had been common along the main rivers, especially the Fox. Many of them were changed into paper mills, as paper manufacturers began to take advantage of Wisconsin's abundant lumber and flowing water. Lumberjacks in the vast Northwoods cut down the ancient white pines, the tallest trees east of the Rockies. From 1850 to 1920, northern Wisconsin became a hive of logging and lumbering.

The lumber industry wasn't dependent on trees alone. Wisconsin's rivers transported cut logs to sawmills, which were powered by the same rivers. In 1851, Wisconsin got its first railroad. It ran 10 miles (16 km)—from Milwaukee to Waukesha—and expanded steadily after that. Freight trains became another means of transporting logs.

In 1881, Frederick Weyerhaeuser, a German-born mill owner in Illinois, bought thousands of acres in northern Wisconsin and the right to cut trees on many more. His company and others like his cut down

nearly all the original forests. When lumber companies depleted the tree supply, they sold the land to immigrants, who hoped to start farms. However, the land was useless for farming—too many tree stumps and too much poor soil. The disappointed immigrants lost out.

In 1872, a settler named Nathaniel Moore discovered a deposit of iron ore 80 miles (130 km) long in the far north. It stretched from Lake Gogebic in Michigan to Namekagon Lake in Wisconsin and was first mined in 1884. At the end of the century, immigrants, including many Italians, came to work dozens of mines in the Gogebic Iron Range.

Logging has long been a an important industry in the northern woods of Wisconsin. Here, a logger stands with a stack of white pine logs near the Menominee Indian Reservation in 1909.

In just one year, 1892, Wisconsin sawmills produced enough lumber to build the equivalent of more than 400,000 three-bedroom houses of today.

Mining was a successful industry in Wisconsin in the early 20th century.

PESHTIGO IN PERIL

By October 8, 1871, months of heat and drought had dried out the brush that lumberjacks had left in the Northwoods. On that day, small fires started near the village of Peshtigo, near Green Bay. The fires joined together and swirled through the former forestland and the villages in it. At least 2,400 people died, including 800 in Peshtigo, before the rain and the shores of Green Bay put the fire out. There's no way to have an accurate death toll because many people lived in the forests where no one knew them or could report them missing.

During this period of industrial growth, German immigrants brought large-scale beer making, or brewing, to the United States, and the railroad gave them access to a national market. Jacob Best started what would later be known as the Pabst Brewing Company in Milwaukee in 1844 as a small neighborhood brewery. His son-in-law, Frederick Pabst, later became president of the company and provided its well-known name. By 1892, it was one of the largest brewers in the United States. Miller Brewing started in 1855, and became even bigger than Pabst in the 20th century. Smaller breweries still exist, including Jacob Leinenkugel of Chippewa Falls (started in 1867).

With all this growth, the state's workforce expanded. Workers united to negotiate with their employers for more pay, shorter workdays, and safer mines and factories. Riots broke out when these negotiations failed. In Milwaukee, people who believed that government should control industry for the benefit of the workers formed a socialist political party. Milwaukee's Victor Berger was a founder of the National Socialist Party, and helped many socialists win seats in local government. In 1910, he became the first socialist elected to the U.S. Congress.

A campaign poster for Socialist leader Victor Berger of Milwaukee

READ ABOUT

Robert M.
La Follette
campaigns in
Cumberland
in 1897.

1933

*The Wisconsin CCC
begins to plant more
than 265 million trees*

▲1950s

*Joseph McCarthy
accuses many citizens
of being communists*

▲1966

*Jesús Salás leads
Hispanic workers in a
protest march*

CHAPTER FIVE

MORE MODERN TIMES

★

THE 20TH CENTURY BEGAN ON AN OPTIMISTIC NOTE, WITH A NATIONAL MOVEMENT TO END POVERTY, HELP WORKING PEOPLE, AND STOP CORRUPTION IN GOVERNMENT. Robert M. La Follette (1855–1925), a congressman and then governor of Wisconsin, led this effort, called the Progressive movement.

1975
The Menominee regain their rights and land

◄**1979**
Milwaukee schools are desegregated

2012
Shootings in Oak Creek and Brookfield leave several people dead

The federal government set up various projects to put jobless men to work during the Great Depression. These workers are improving a county road near Westfield.

WORLD WAR I

In 1914, Germany went to war against other European nations. Some Americans were opposed to joining Europe's war. But when the United States entered the conflict in 1917, many Wisconsinites enlisted to help America and its allies toward victory in 1918. At about this time, Wisconsin became a national leader in the development of radio, or "wireless" transmissions. Researchers in the state were responsible for important innovations that improved communications for millions of people.

THE GREAT DEPRESSION

The 1920s seemed promising for Wisconsin. Industry was booming. Americans looked to the state for aluminum pots and pans, fountain pens, bathroom fixtures—

all sorts of wares. Then the New York Stock Exchange crashed in 1929. Businesses and banks closed, and people lost their jobs. The Great Depression was just beginning.

In 1932, Americans elected Franklin D. Roosevelt president, hoping he could fix the country's economic disaster. In a program called the New Deal, he persuaded Congress to create jobs for people. Nationwide, more than 3 million workers in the Civilian Conservation Corps (CCC) planted trees, repaired wildlife habitats, built roads through parks and forests, cleaned streams, and built fences. The workers received a check every month, most of which went to their families at home while they lived in workers' camps. The 165,000 workers of the CCC in Wisconsin planted 265 million trees between 1933 and 1942. During the Depression, milk prices were so low that Wisconsin dairy farmers spent their savings to run their farms. In 1932, some farmers joined forces to go on strike. They dumped their milk on the ground rather than sell it for such low prices.

MINI-BIO

EARLE M. TERRY: RADIO PIONEER

As a professor at the University of Wisconsin—Madison, Earle Melvin Terry (1869–1929) helped bring about voice broadcasts—rather than Morse code—and expanded the range of radio transmission. Working with physicist Edward Bennett, Terry developed 9XM, a transmitting station that kept isolated rural people informed about local and world news. The station later had programs designed for use in schools. "Afield with Ranger Mac" was broadcast from 1933 to 1954. Each week, host Wakelin McNeel would answer students' letters and give his views on conservation and nature. McNeel often discussed soil erosion and forestry with his young listeners, two important issues to the people of Wisconsin.

? **Want to know more?** Visit www.factsfornow .scholastic.com and enter the keyword **Wisconsin**.

During the Great Depression, many farmers faced hard times. This Wisconsin family gets financial advice from a Farm Security Administration official.

FACING WORLD WAR II

With the help of the federal and state programs, Wisconsinites survived the Great Depression. When World War II erupted in Europe in 1939, many people began to recover financially as the conflict called for weapons and supplies that created jobs for U.S. citizens. In 1941, Japan bombed Pearl Harbor, Hawai'i, and the United States entered the war. More than 300,000 men and women from Wisconsin served in the U.S. Army, Navy, and Army Air Corps. Thousands more worked in war-related industries at home.

The Manitowoc Shipbuilding Company hoped to build destroyers for the U.S. Navy, so the firm was surprised when the navy offered it a contract to build submarines.

Up to that time, a firm in Connecticut had built all the U.S. submarines. The Manitowoc company had to learn how to make them. To test the boats, they were launched sideways and submerged in the deepest part of Lake Michigan. Each submarine was transported on a barge down the Chicago River, through the Illinois Waterway, to the Mississippi River, and then to New Orleans. The 7,000 employees of Manitowoc Shipbuilding produced 28 submarines that helped win the war in the Pacific.

Thousands of German and Japanese prisoners of war (POWs) passed through Camp McCoy near Sparta. They worked throughout the state harvesting crops, cutting trees for paper pulp, and tending dairies. The U.S. and its allies won the war in 1945, and all former prisoners left the state by early 1946.

SEE IT HERE!

USS *COBIA*

The Wisconsin Maritime Museum at Manitowoc features the USS *Cobia*, a submarine just like the ones the Manitowoc Shipbuilding Company produced during World War II. You can even spend a night on board.

The Kenosha Comets were one team in the All-American Girls Professional Baseball League.

TAKING THE FIELD

With his players at war, Chicago Cubs owner Philip K. Wrigley (who lived in Lake Geneva) created the All-American Girls Professional Baseball League. It started in 1943 with four teams, including Wisconsin's Racine Belles and Kenosha Comets. The Milwaukee Chicks joined them later. The league ended in 1954.

During the 1950s, Senator Joseph McCarthy accused many people of being communists and fueled a fear of communism in the United States.

WORD TO KNOW

communism *a system in which all property and goods are owned by everyone and controlled by the government*

THE COLD WAR

The Soviet Union (now Russia) had been an ally of the United States during World War II, but when U.S. troops left Europe, Soviet troops stayed and forcibly took over several countries. For the next 35 years, in what was known as the cold war, the United States and the Soviet Union remained at odds over their different forms of government and economic systems.

During this period of tension, many Americans began to fear **communism**. They worried that the Soviets would take away their personal freedoms. Propaganda on both sides fed such fears. Then, in the 1950s, Wisconsin's Republican senator, Joseph McCarthy, began to turn people's fear of communism into hysteria in what was later seen as an effort to gain attention and political power. He accused dozens of people in government of secretly belonging to the Communist Party and influencing the nation's foreign policy. He had no proof, but the accused often had few ways of defending themselves.

He went on to accuse well-known people, such as actors and writers, of being communists, or communist sympathizers. Some people lost their jobs. Some members of the press were afraid to say anything against McCarthy, for fear that they, too, would be accused. Eventually, McCarthy's Senate hearings were broadcast on live television. The American public saw firsthand the way McCarthy bullied and threatened witnesses. Most people no longer took his charges seriously, and soon he lost all his influence. Today, the word "McCarthyism" is used to describe tactics involving personal attacks and false accusations against individuals to defame their character.

THE GREAT MIGRATION

After World War II, Wisconsin's population changed dramatically. In what came to be called the Great Migration, hundreds of thousands of African Americans from the rural South moved to industrial cities of the North. Between 1945 and 1960, Wisconsin's African American population increased 600 percent, most of it in Milwaukee.

The new black residents of Milwaukee tried to find places to live. But many landlords would not rent apartments or houses to them. African Americans were forced to live in racially **segregated**, or separated, areas. Some African Americans had good jobs in industry, but whites did not allow them to live outside the area called the Inner Core or to go to school in white neighborhoods.

In 1954, the U.S. Supreme Court ruled that segregated schools were unconstitutional. The Court required all school systems to set about desegregating schools "with all deliberate speed."

WORD TO KNOW

segregated *separated from another group, usually by race or gender*

FATHER JAMES GROPPI: CIVIL RIGHTS ACTIVIST

A Catholic priest, Father James Groppi (1930–1985) marched and demonstrated to promote open housing and enforcement of civil rights laws in Milwaukee, as well as in the South. Notably, he led rallies for several consecutive nights in Milwaukee in 1967 to highlight segregation in the city, leading participants out of black neighborhoods and into those that were predominantly white.

❓ Want to know more? Visit www.factsfornow .scholastic.com and enter the keyword **Wisconsin**.

Milwaukee didn't move quickly enough. In 1979, 25 years after school segregation was declared unconstitutional, the courts finally ordered the school board to desegregate its schools. Black children were bused to schools in the predominantly white suburbs, and white children were bused into largely black urban neighborhoods.

Segregated housing was also a problem all over the nation. People of color sought the full rights of citizenship that white people had—such as living wherever they chose. They had been denied that right, especially in the South, for many decades.

Father James Groppi leads a group of people protesting school segregation in Milwaukee.

FAIR HOUSING

On a hot July night in 1967, police tried to break up a fight in a tavern in the Inner Core. It turned into an angry riot over housing, and four people were killed. Several weeks later, the Milwaukee Common Council failed to pass a law giving African Americans the right to live where they wanted, a concept called open housing. During the following weeks, black and white civil rights activists organized marches. In the spring of 1968, the federal government declared housing discrimination illegal, and the Milwaukee Common Council finally complied with the law.

Many white people moved to the suburbs, leaving the inner city to African Americans. In 2004, a study found that many black people still lived in poor, racially segregated parts of Milwaukee. Now, instead of being segregated by law, a lack of opportunities and economic disadvantages keep many people in these neighborhoods.

MORE TROUBLES FOR NATIVE AMERICANS

In the 1950s, Congress stopped providing economic support to Native Americans on reservations. Congress thought that doing so would help to end a cycle of poverty on reservations and encourage Indians to join mainstream America.

Congress created a plan called termination that was designed to gradually cut all support from the U.S. government to Native American groups. The first group to be terminated was the Menominee of Wisconsin. Because there were large forests on the Menominee reservation, government officials thought the people would become financially independent by cutting trees and selling lumber. The federal government converted

Secretary of the Interior Rogers Morton signs documents restoring tribal status to the Menominee Native Americans in 1975.

WORD TO KNOW

developers *people who change natural areas into land used for houses or businesses*

the large reservation into a state county and created a corporation to run the affairs of the group. Termination took effect in 1961.

Termination did not work out the way officals had hoped. Within a few years, individuals had to sell their homes to outside **developers** because they couldn't afford to pay their taxes. Hospitals and schools failed. People lost jobs at their own lumber mill. The termination policy was a failure, and Indian poverty became even worse. Menominee County became the poorest county in the state.

Led by Ada E. Deer, activists formed Determination of Rights and Unity for Menominee Shareholders (DRUMS). DRUMS protests, including a 222-mile (357 km) march to Madison, led to the end of termination in 1975. The Menominee were once again a nation, with all the rights and land they had had before.

RIGHTS FOR WISCONSIN'S LATINOS

Latino migrant workers had been coming into Wisconsin to work in agriculture and industry for half a century, but their numbers greatly increased during World War II. Most were of Mexican heritage and came from the southwestern United States. They picked cherries, corn, and other vegetables, and dug potatoes for low wages.

In 1966, a student at the University of Wisconsin–Madison, Jesús Salás, led Hispanic workers on a march from Wautoma to Madison to protest the working conditions for migrant laborers. He founded a union for farmworkers and negotiated minimum wages for them. Crop picking is now largely done with machinery, but about 4,000 workers still come into the state each year during the harvest to pick crops that machines can damage. Many large dairy farms today also rely on low-paid immigrant workers.

Many of the Hispanics who first came as seasonal farmworkers have settled in Wisconsin. Even greater numbers of Hispanics live and work in the cities.

21ST CENTURY CHALLENGES

The worldwide economic crisis from 2007 to 2009 hit Wisconsin hard. Thousands of workers lost their jobs. The loss of income pushed many residents into poverty, which often resulted in the loss of health insurance coverage. Wisconsin responded with aggressive plans to stimulate business development and job growth. By mid-2013, the number of nonfarm jobs was growing at its highest rate in 20 years. As the economy continues to improve, people in Wisconsin are looking toward the future with hope and optimism.

Workers at a garden center

READ ABOUT

University of Wisconsin Badgers fans cheer on their football team during a game against the Arizona State Sun Devils.

PEOPLE PEOPLE PEOPLE PEOPLE PEOPLE

CHAPTER SIX

PEOPLE

★

NEW PEOPLE ARRIVE IN WISCONSIN EVERY DAY. On July 1, 2012, an estimated 5,726,398 people lived in the state—a 0.7 percent increase from the 2010 census. But there's still plenty of room. With a population density of about 105 persons per square mile (41 per sq km), Wisconsin is the 26th least crowded state in the country. Most of Wisconsin's population is in the southeastern part of the state. The north is the least populated, with parts of that area having fewer than 10 people per square mile (4 per sq km).

A new housing development going up near Milwaukee

Big City Life

This list shows the population of Wisconsin's biggest cities.

Milwaukee	.594,833
Madison	.233,209
Green Bay	.104,057
Kenosha	.99,218
Racine	.78,860

Source: U.S. Census Bureau, 2010 census

CITY AND COUNTRY

According to 2010 estimates, more people lived in rural areas of Wisconsin than at any other time—but the percentage compared to the entire population had shrunk. Today, the rural population is about 1.5 million, with most people living in small towns, not on farms. While the number of farms has shrunk by three-fourths from 100 years ago, the remaining farms are much larger, so most of the state's land is still farmland.

The least densely populated county in 2010 was Iron County, with only 4 people per square mile (1.5 per sq km), for a total of 5,916 people in the county, which was down from the 2000 census. The most densely populated is Milwaukee County (which includes the city of Milwaukee), with 947,735 people, or 3,929 people per square mile (1,517 per sq km). Its population increased by roughly 1 percent since 2000.

Where Wisconsinites Live

The colors on this map indicate population density throughout the state.
The darker the color, the more people live there.

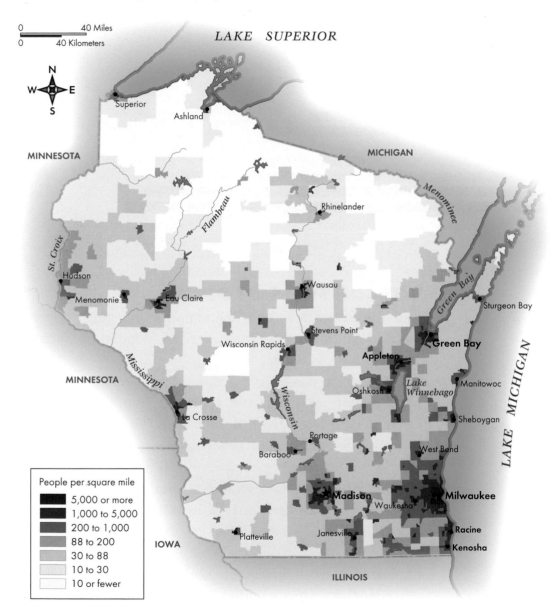

0   40 Miles
0   40 Kilometers

N
W   E
S

LAKE SUPERIOR

MINNESOTA

MICHIGAN

Superior

Ashland

Rhinelander

Flambeau

St. Croix

Menominee

Green Bay

Hudson

Wausau

Sturgeon Bay

Menomonie

Eau Claire

Stevens Point

Green Bay

Wisconsin Rapids

Appleton

MINNESOTA

Mississippi

Oshkosh

Lake Winnebago

Manitowoc

LAKE MICHIGAN

La Crosse

Wisconsin

Sheboygan

Portage

West Bend

Baraboo

Madison

Milwaukee

Waukesha

People per square mile

- 5,000 or more
- 1,000 to 5,000
- 200 to 1,000
- 88 to 200
- 30 to 88
- 10 to 30
- 10 or fewer

IOWA

Platteville

Janesville

Racine

Kenosha

ILLINOIS

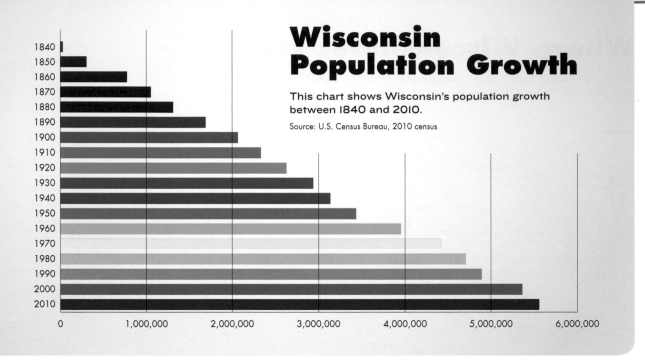

Wisconsin Population Growth

This chart shows Wisconsin's population growth between 1840 and 2010.

Source: U.S. Census Bureau, 2010 census

WISCONSIN'S PEOPLE

Native Americans remain a vital part of the state's population. Wisconsin's Native American population ranks 16th among all states.

Wisconsin has been a destination for many foreign-born people. Wisconsin is home to many people of German and Norwegian descent, and to more people of Polish ancestry than any other state. People from more than 60 ethnic groups live in the state, including Albanian, Slovene, Portuguese, Filipino, and Hmong.

The first Mexicans arrived in Wisconsin as early as 1850. Their numbers remained low until the 1920s, when they began coming from the American Southwest by the thousands to work on sugar beet farms and in factories.

Hispanics are the fastest-growing ethnic group in Wisconsin. The Hispanic population increased more than 74 percent between 2000 and 2010. Today, about 5.9 percent of the state's people are Hispanic, and about

People QuickFacts

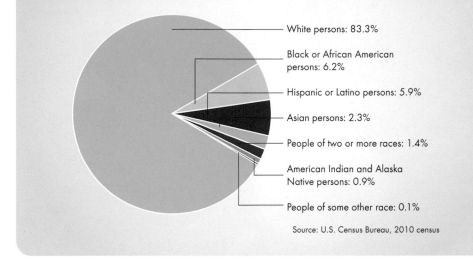

White persons: 83.3%

Black or African American persons: 6.2%

Hispanic or Latino persons: 5.9%

Asian persons: 2.3%

People of two or more races: 1.4%

American Indian and Alaska Native persons: 0.9%

People of some other race: 0.1%

Source: U.S. Census Bureau, 2010 census

60 percent of them are of Mexican origin. Almost half of them live in Milwaukee. About 11 percent of the people in neighboring Racine, Kenosha, and Walworth Counties are Hispanic.

In recent years, many Amish people from Pennsylvania have moved to central Wisconsin, fleeing the spreading suburbs of Philadelphia and Washington, D.C., for Wisconsin's more affordable rural areas. Called Old Order Amish, these people, who are of German ancestry, maintain lives with few modern conveniences. Their black horse-drawn buggies are often seen on the roads surrounding their communities.

There are 11 official Indian reservations in Wisconsin. The gambling and tourism industries have helped the Oneida begin to buy all the land within the boundaries of their reservation.

The Potawatomi were left out when reservations were formed in 1854, but in the 20th century, they bought separate pieces of land in Forest County. They were very poor until the government passed the Indian Reorganization Act in 1934, and they began to receive some federal money. When the Potawatomi were

STOLEN CULTURE

The federal government decided in the late 1800s that the easiest way to control the Indians was to teach them European ways. Native American children were taken away from their families and sent to boarding schools, where they were not allowed to sing or dance or speak their own languages. Many groups today have only a few people who speak traditional languages and know the dances.

Each week, students at the Lac Courte Oreilles High School gather in the gym for a powwow organized to reinforce the Ojibwe culture and language.

allowed to develop casinos on Indian lands, especially in Milwaukee, they began to earn money.

The Mole Lake Ojibwe were promised 12 square miles (31 sq km) of land in 1854, but they received nothing until 1934. Then they were given less than 3 square miles (8 sq km).

EDUCATION

Wisconsin has always placed a great emphasis on education. In addition to learning at traditional schools, a growing number of students are schooled at home. Wisconsin law requires that homeschooled students receive 875 hours of instruction each school year. That includes reading textbooks, as well as participating in field trips, using computers, and learning skills such as cooking, driving, or home repair.

The first place in the United States to have a kindergarten was Watertown. Margarethe Meyer Schurz learned about early education for children (*kinder*) while traveling in Germany. She started a kindergarten in 1856.

The University of Wisconsin was founded when Wisconsin became a state in 1848. Today, it is a statewide system with 13 four-year universities and 13 two-year colleges. The system educates a large percentage of Wisconsin's college students and is an internationally recognized research center. Marquette University is the largest private school in the state, and Carroll College in Waukesha is the state's oldest college, founded as an academy in 1841, and becoming a college in 1846. Graduates of Yale University in Connecticut founded Beloit College also in 1846. Founded in 1849, Lawrence University in Appleton became the state's first college to admit women.

The College of the Menominee Nation began in 1993. It now holds classes both in Keshena, the county/reservation seat, and in Green Bay. The Lac Courte Oreilles Ojibwe also have a community college, located in Hayward.

MINI-BIO   73

FRANK LLOYD WRIGHT: FAMED ARCHITECT

Born in Richland Center, Frank Lloyd Wright (1867–1959) was one of the most influential architects of all time. He is best remembered for his contributions to the modern movement in architecture. By the end of his career, he had designed more than 400 buildings. You can see Wright buildings in Madison, Delavan, and Milwaukee, as well as the spectacular S. C. Johnson Wax building in Racine. You can even spend the night at a beautiful limestone home Wright designed for himself near Spring Green.

❓ **Want to know more?** Visit www.factsfornow.scholastic.com and enter the keyword **Wisconsin**.

The University of Wisconsin student union patio is on the shores of beautiful Lake Mendota.

HOW TO TALK LIKE A WISCONSINITE

There are some rules for talking in Wisconsin, or "'Sconsin," as many natives say it. Try out these words and phrases, so everyone will think you're a real Wisconsinite.

Bubbler: A drinking fountain

Flatlander: Someone from outside the state, especially Illinois

Sheepshead, or sheephead: A card game that's comprehensible only to a Wisconsinite

Stop-and-go lights: Traffic lights

HOW TO EAT LIKE A WISCONSINITE

When you think of special Wisconsin foods, you probably think first of cheese. Why else would Green Bay Packers fans wear cheese-wedge hats and be called cheeseheads? But, you'll also find great fruits and vegetables, along with hearty meat dishes. See the next page for a sample.

Bratwurst with sauerkraut

MENU
WHAT'S ON THE MENU IN WISCONSIN?

★ ★ ★

Cranberries

The Brat
Wisconsinites adore a brat (braht), especially while tailgating at Packers or Brewers games. Short for bratwurst, this spicy sausage brought by German and Polish immigrants is often simmered first and then cooked on a charcoal grill. Put it in a bun with mustard, sauerkraut, and onions, and savor the flavor.

Pasties
Pasties (PASS-tees) are self-contained meals that were were brought to Wisconsin by English miners. They consist of folded piecrust containing meat, potatoes, and vegetables. The miners carried them to work in their pockets and ate them cold. Today, they are most often served hot.

Cheese Curds
Curds are what cheese is before it is pressed into a cheese shape. You can eat them right out of the package or battered and fried. Fresh curds squeak when you bite into them.

Fish Boils
You can find them in lots of places, but Door County is famous for this treat of whitefish cooked outdoors in a steaming pot of vegetables. The meal is traditionally topped off with a piece of Door County cherry pie.

TRY THIS RECIPE
Wild Rice Cranberry Salad
Wisconsin grows more cranberries than any other state. The Menominee ("people of the wild rice") and other Native Americans have harvested Wisconsin's wild rice for centuries. Put these two Wisconsin staples together and you've got yourself a tasty treat to eat at home or on a picnic. Be sure to have an adult nearby to help.

Ingredients:
1 cup uncooked wild rice
½ cup celery, chopped
½ cup dried cranberries
½ cup green peppers, chopped
¼ cup green onions, sliced
¼ cup fresh parsley, chopped
¼ cup white vinegar
½ cup cranberry juice
1 tablespoon olive oil
1 teaspoon dried basil
2 tablespoons sugar
1 teaspoon salt

Instructions:
1. Cook wild rice according to package directions. Put it in a medium mixing bowl to cool.
2. Add to the cooled wild rice: celery, cranberries, green peppers, green onions, and parsley.
3. In a small mixing bowl, whisk the white vinegar, cranberry juice, olive oil, basil, sugar, and salt until everything is combined.
4. Add this dressing to the wild rice mixture. Toss lightly.
5. Put salad in the refrigerator. Once it's chilled, it's ready to eat!

ARTISTS AND WRITERS

Wisconsin is home to many artists. Native American arts include porcupine quill decorations on birch bark and beaded costumes, both created by Ojibwe craftspeople, as well as cornhusk dolls made by Oneida women.

The Hmong create exquisite needlework, called *paj ntaub* (pronounced "pon dow"), which means "flower cloth." Intricate and colorful wall hangings and quilts show animal scenes and geometric designs, usually on black fabric. Hmong "story cloths" tell the story of their migration from Vietnam to America and related events.

Women at a local Wisconsin festival. The Hmong people are known for their intricate beadwork.

HMONG MEANS "FREE PEOPLE"

The people called the Hmong (pronounced "mung") are the descendants of people who settled long ago in the mountains of Southeast Asia. During the Vietnam War, many Hmong people in Laos and Vietnam supported the United States. When U.S. troops withdrew, leaving the whole of Vietnam to the communists, many of those who had aided the United States fled. Many Hmong ended up in Wisconsin. Gradually, members of their extended families came to Wisconsin, primarily in Milwaukee and around Wausau, Appleton, and Green Bay. By 2010, Wisconsin's Hmong population had reached 49,240. The state has one of the largest Hmong populations in the country.

Other crafts include decorated eggs from eastern European countries and rosemaling, which is a Norwegian art involving a special kind of painting, usually flowers on wooden objects or walls. Amish quilt making and woodworking are becoming popular as Amish communities grow.

Wisconsinite Frank O. King's comic strip, *Gasoline Alley*, first appeared in newspapers in 1918 and can still be seen in some papers today, although King died in 1959.

A number of Wisconsin writers have won the prestigious Pulitzer Prize. Edna Ferber of Appleton won the 1924 prize for *So Big*. Madison-born Thornton Wilder won three Pulitzer Prizes: for the novel *The Bridge of San Luis Rey* in 1927, the play *Our Town* in 1938, and the play *The Skin of Our Teeth* in 1942. The musical *Hello, Dolly* was based on his play *The Matchmaker*.

Wisconsin's writers for young people have drawn heavily on the state's scenery and stories. *Caddie Woodlawn*, written by Carol Ryrie Brink in 1935, takes place on the western Wisconsin frontier. Laura Ingalls Wilder is remembered for the stories she wrote about her own life. Her Little House books first appeared in the 1930s and 1940s. Then there's *Rascal* (1963), a book about a pet raccoon that author Sterling North of Edgerton raised as a boy. North's novel *Midnight and Jeremiah* became a Disney movie, *So Dear to My Heart,* in 1949.

THE MUSIC SCENE

Les Paul, a jazz musician, was born in Waukesha and developed the solid-body electric guitar. The Gibson "Les Paul" model, designed in 1952, is one of the most revered guitars in the industry. Paul went on to influence a number of musicians,

Guitar legend
Les Paul

including Milwaukee-born Steve Miller. One of Miller's best-known songs is "Fly Like an Eagle" (1976). Woody Herman, also from Milwaukee, was a jazz clarinetist and a big-band leader.

Wisconsin has a rich folk music heritage. Pee Wee King was a country music star of the 1930s and 1940s known for "The Tennessee Waltz" and "You Belong to Me." He was born in Milwaukee and lived in Abrams.

GOOD SPORTS

Almost all Wisconsinites have a deep respect for their Green Bay Packers. Founded by E. L. "Curly" Lambeau in 1919, the Packers got their name from the first players, who were employed by Indian Packing Corp. The Packers are the only team in the National Football

Legendary Green Bay Packers coach Vince Lombardi celebrates a victory at Lambeau Field in 1965.

League (NFL) not located in a big city. To survive financially, the team had to become a nonprofit corporation and sell shares to local residents. So the people of Green Bay own the Packers.

The Packers began their winning ways under the legendary Vince Lombardi, who took the head coaching job in 1958. Within three years, the Packers became NFL champions. Before he retired in 1967, Lombardi had led the Packers to the first two Super Bowl championships. The Packers later repeated as Super Bowl champs in the 1996 and 2010 seasons.

The Milwaukee Brewers of baseball's National League play in Miller Park, which opened in 2001. The Brewers were created after the Milwaukee Braves moved to Atlanta, taking slugger Hank Aaron with them. Aaron hit most of his home runs in Milwaukee in the late 1950s and early 1960s before moving to Atlanta with the Braves and breaking Babe Ruth's home-run record.

Bicycling is also a popular sport in the Badger State. When the state paved roads for milk trucks in the 20th century, it created ideal conditions for cycling. Today, cyclists who come to Wisconsin marvel at its clean, well-maintained roadways.

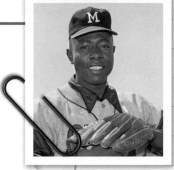

MINI-BIO

HENRY "HANK" AARON: HOME-RUN KING

Henry "Hank" Aaron was born in Alabama in 1934. He started playing professional baseball in 1951 with a Negro League team, the Indianapolis Clowns. A scout for the Milwaukee Braves invited him to Wisconsin. He played for the Braves' farm club, the Eau Claire Bears, and in 1954 moved on to the Major League Milwaukee Braves. He hit home run after home run for Milwaukee and helped them win the World Series in 1957. The Braves later moved to Atlanta. In 1974, he broke Babe Ruth's home-run record. Aaron came back to Milwaukee and played one season with the Brewers. He was inducted into the National Baseball Hall of Fame in 1982. Aaron's record went unbroken until 2007.

? Want to know more? Visit www.factsfornow.scholastic.com and enter the keyword **Wisconsin**.

READ ABOUT

Wisconsin's state capitol

CHAPTER SEVEN

GOVERNMENT

★

"**W**E, THE PEOPLE OF WISCONSIN . . . DO ESTABLISH THIS CONSTITUTION. All people are born equally free and independent, and have certain inherent rights; among these are life, liberty, and the pursuit of happiness; to secure these rights, governments are instituted, deriving their just powers from the consent of the governed." These are the opening words of the Wisconsin Constitution, which establishes the rights of citizens and the powers and responsibilities of the state government.

LOTS OF CAPITOLS

Belmont, in the southwest corner of the state, was the capital of Wisconsin Territory for 46 days in 1836. But the first territorial governor, Henry Dodge, did most of his business in nearby Mineral Point. He ordered the construction of a capitol, called the Council House, and a supreme court from a builder in Pennsylvania. The two buildings were brought to Belmont by steamboat. (The first wooden capitol is no longer used but can be toured at First Capitol State Park.)

When statehood was drawing near, Belmont lost out to a more centrally located site. James Doty, about to become the second territorial governor, chose a narrow band of land (called an isthmus) he owned between several small lakes. He named the new capital for the fourth president of the United States, James Madison.

The first capitol in Madison was too small soon after it opened in 1838. A larger domed building was ready in 1869, but even it was too small, so in 1882 the legislature voted to add two wings.

The Wisconsin state capitol

Capital City

This map shows places of interest in Madison, Wisconsin's capital city.

As a larger building was being discussed in 1904, fire destroyed the capitol. Construction of the newer one started right away, and by 1909 the legislature was able to start meeting in one wing. The capitol eventually had four wings extending from the largest state capitol dome in the United States. It was finally completed in 1917. But because the country was at war in Europe, the building wasn't dedicated until 1965!

Atop the dome is Daniel C. French's golden statue of a female figure, called *Wisconsin*. She stands 15 feet

Capitol Facts

Here are some interesting facts about Wisconsin's state capitol.

Height . . . . .284.4 feet (86.7 m) high, just 3 feet (less than 1 m) shorter than the U.S. Capitol in Washington, D.C.
Number of stories 4
Each of 4 wings:
   Width .125 feet (38 m)
   Height . . . . 84 feet (25.6 m)
   Length . . . . .187 feet (57 m)
Construction dates 1905–1917
Construction cost (1909) . . . . $7.2 million
Renovation cost (1990) . . . . $18.9 million
Surrounding park . . . . .13.4 acres (5.4 ha)

Forty-three varieties of stone from all over the world were used to build the state capitol.

The statue *Wisconsin* atop the capital dome

5 inches (4.7 m) tall and weighs more than 3 tons. She has a badger on her helmet. The inside of the huge dome, 200 feet (60 m) overhead, is painted with a vast mural called *Resources of Wisconsin*, by Edwin Howland Blashfield.

HOW WISCONSIN WORKS

Wisconsin is divided into 72 counties. The largest by population is Milwaukee, and the smallest is Menominee, an Indian reservation. The largest in geographic area is Marathon, and the smallest is Pepin. The state is also divided into 33 legislative districts. Each one elects representatives to the state government. The state government is constructed like the federal government, with three branches: executive, legislative, and judicial.

Blashfield's *Resources of Wisconsin*, inside the capitol dome

Wisconsin Counties

This map shows the 72 counties in Wisconsin.
Madison, the state capital, is indicated with a star.

LAKE SUPERIOR

MINNESOTA

MICHIGAN

DOUGLAS
BAYFIELD
ASHLAND
IRON
VILAS
BURNETT
WASHBURN
SAWYER
FLORENCE
PRICE
ONEIDA
FOREST
POLK
BARRON
RUSK
MARINETTE
LINCOLN
LANGLADE
TAYLOR
ST. CROIX
CHIPPEWA
DUNN
MENOMINEE
OCONTO
MARATHON
PIERCE
EAU CLAIRE
CLARK
SHAWANO
PEPIN
DOOR
Green Bay
BUFFALO
WOOD
PORTAGE
WAUPACA
BROWN
TREMPEALEAU
JACKSON
OUTAGAMIE
KEWAUNEE
MINNESOTA
WINNEBAGO
CALUMET
MANITOWOC
WAUSHARA
ADAMS
LA CROSSE
MONROE
JUNEAU
MARQUETTE
GREEN
LAKE
SHEBOYGAN
FOND DU LAC
LAKE MICHIGAN
VERNON
WASHINGTON
OZAUKEE
RICHLAND
SAUK
COLUMBIA
DODGE
CRAWFORD
Madison
Milwaukee
IOWA
DANE
JEFFERSON
WAUKESHA
MILWAUKEE
GRANT
IOWA
LAFAYETTE
GREEN
ROCK
WALWORTH
RACINE
KENOSHA

ILLINOIS

0   40 Miles
0   40 Kilometers

N
W   E
S

County boundary

Wisconsin's State Government

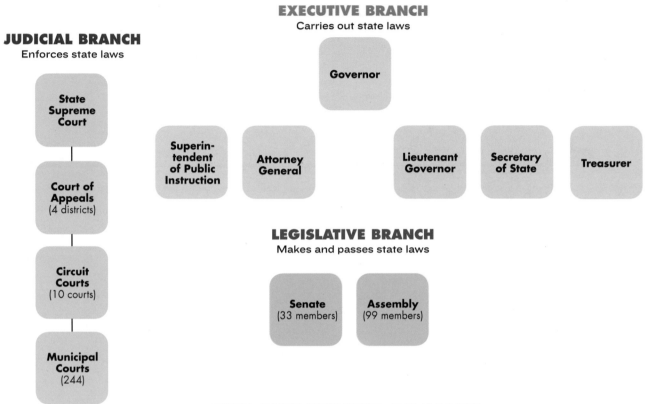

EXECUTIVE BRANCH
Carries out state laws

Governor

Superintendent of Public Instruction

Attorney General

Lieutenant Governor

Secretary of State

Treasurer

JUDICIAL BRANCH
Enforces state laws

State Supreme Court

Court of Appeals (4 districts)

Circuit Courts (10 courts)

Municipal Courts (244)

LEGISLATIVE BRANCH
Makes and passes state laws

Senate (33 members)

Assembly (99 members)

THE EXECUTIVE BRANCH

The governor and lieutenant governor lead the executive branch. Both of them are elected to four-year terms. The governor appoints people to other leadership positions and helps to create the state budget. The budget determines what things the government will pay for and how it will get the necessary money (mostly through taxes).

One memorable governor was Robert M. La Follette. He started primary elections so that the state's citizens could choose their candidates, instead of them being chosen by political parties, which were often corrupt. He set rules for powerful industries and developed a program to pay workers injured on the job. In 1906, the state legislature elected La Follette to the U.S.

The Wisconsin Assembly in session

Senate. In Washington, he persuaded Congress to let the people directly elect senators, an idea that became the Seventeenth Amendment to the Constitution.

THE LEGISLATIVE BRANCH

The legislative branch makes laws for the state. Wisconsin's legislature consists of a senate and an assembly. The senate has 33 seats, one from each legislative district. The assembly has 99 seats, three from each district. Senators are elected to four-year terms, and the assembly representatives are elected for two-year terms.

Wisconsin lawmakers drew national attention in the early 2010s. The issue was collective bargaining, the process of negotiations between workers and their employers to regulate working conditions, such as health benefits and pensions. In 2011, Republican governor Scott Walker signed a bill, called Act 10, that would take away the collective bargaining rights of state government workers. He did this to help save

A Vote on Act 10?

PRO

Act 10 stripped away collective bargaining for most unionized public workers, including teachers, in Wisconsin. It also requires workers to contribute about 6 percent of their retirement pensions and about 13 percent of their health care costs. Many school districts immediately reported large savings because they were paying millions of dollars less of teachers' health insurance and pension costs. The Madison Metropolitan School District reported that it would save $18.6 million in the 2012–13 school year alone. Other districts reported significant savings as well. "The bottom line is that Act 10 allows school boards to take control of their budgets without union interference and act in the best interests of their students," said Madison district superintendent Dan Nerad.

CON

The introduction of Act 10 resulted in a divided and bitter political climate in Wisconsin. Teachers who opposed the new law claim that it is unfair. After all, they argue, the teachers' union in Wisconsin negotiated for what they received over the years, and now Act 10 has taken many of those gains away. Speaking about the teachers' opposition to Act 10, however, Waukesha school superintendent Todd Gray said, "If we have teachers concerned and morale is low, that hurts us." Many also argue that Act 10 is an attempt to break up unions in the state. Labor expert Frank Emspak said, "It's really an assault on the democratic process in the workplace. All of these things result in a lessening of the ability of people in the workplace to speak on a level playing field with their employer."

the state millions of dollars by paying less for workers' health insurance, retirement, and sick leave.

When Act 10 went to the state legislature for approval, 14 Senate Democrats fled Wisconsin and traveled to Illinois in order to delay a vote. The senators were threatened with fines and loss of salary. Senate Republicans called for the arrest of the absent senators, but Wisconsin law enforcement officials were not allowed to cross state lines into Illinois. After making small changes to the bill, the Senate passed the new collective bargaining law. The 14 Democratic senators soon returned to Wisconsin.

Workers across the state feared a loss of their rights and immediately protested the new law. Large demonstrations at the capitol in Madison drew hundreds of thousands of angry union members and their supporters. Anti-Walker activists demanded a recall election to remove him from office before his term ended. Walker, however, won the new election and remained in office.

After months of court challenges to the new collective bargaining law, a U.S. court of appeals upheld the law in January 2013. Workers' bargaining rights would be greatly limited.

THE JUDICIAL BRANCH

The state's supreme court heads the judicial branch. The public elects seven justices to the bench for 10-year terms. The court of appeals has 12 justices. These judges listen to cases that have already been tried but are being reconsidered. Below that are more than 200 judges who serve on the local level. The judges in the judicial branch listen to court cases and decide if laws have been broken.

MINI-BIO

VEL PHILLIPS: GOVERNOR WHEN NO ONE WAS LOOKING

Milwaukee-born civil rights leader Vel Phillips (1924—) was the first African American woman to graduate from the University of Wisconsin Law School. When still in her 20s, she ran for elective office (the Milwaukee Public School Board) for the first time. She then held many different elective positions—including several firsts for a black man or woman—all while being an activist in fighting discrimination in housing, education, and jobs. She was elected the first African American judge in the state and then the first woman and African American as secretary of state. In 1978, when the governor and lieutenant governor happened to be away at the same time, Phillips served as acting governor. It was a short stint during a sexist time; Phillips noticed that "the men hurried back" when they realized they had left a woman in charge. In 2004, Phillips led the election campaign of Racine-born Gwen Moore, the first black Wisconsinite elected to the U.S. House of Representatives.

? **Want to know more?** Visit www.factsfornow .scholastic.com and enter the keyword **Wisconsin**.

Students at Hayward Elementary School learn about the Ojibwe culture and language.

In 1974, a 17-year legal controversy began when authorities arrested two Ojibwe brothers for breaking state conservation laws by ice fishing on an off-reservation lake. The arrest led their tribe to sue the state. According to 19th-century treaties, the Ojibwe had agreed to give up their land titles, but kept the right to hunt and fish on the territory. While Wisconsin's judges wrangled with the issue, some non-Indian Wisconsinites spread rumors that the Ojibwe would ruin tourism in the state by hunting all of its fish and game. Some protests turned violent, drawing national media attention. In the fight against racism and rumor, Wisconsin ordered its schools to teach local Indian history, culture, and tribal sovereignty. In 1991, the courts finally granted the Ojibwe their fishing rights.

THE FEDERAL SCENE

In addition to state districts, Wisconsin is divided into eight congressional districts for electing people to the U.S. House of Representatives. Two U.S. senators are elected to represent the state.

The largest federal government facility in Wisconsin is Fort McCoy, in use since 1909. Originally called Camp McCoy, it covers 60,000 acres (24,000 ha) in the west-central part of the state. During World War II, it was a camp for prisoners of war. In 1980, Fort McCoy temporarily served as a resettlement center for about 15,000 Cuban refugees. In the 1990s, it housed homeless veterans. Now, more than 100,000 men and women from many different states train there each year for all branches of the U.S. military. From 2008 to 2010, Fort McCoy sent National Guard and reserve troops into action in Iraq and Afghanistan.

A National Guard unit undergoes checkpoint training at Fort McCoy near Tomah.

Representing Wisconsin

This list shows the number of elected officials who represent Wisconsin, both on the state and national levels.

OFFICE	NUMBER	LENGTH OF TERM
State senators	33	4 years
State assembly members	99	2 years
U.S. senators	2	6 years
U.S. representatives	8	2 years
Presidential electors	10	—

State Flag

The flag of Wisconsin features the state seal on a field of dark blue. The flag was first created in 1863, at the request of Civil War regiments who wanted a flag to fly. The current design was made official in 1913. In 1979, it was altered to add the name of the state above the seal and below it, "1848," the year Wisconsin became a state.

State Seal

The state seal features the state motto, "Forward." Below it is an image of the badger, the state animal. The seal also features a sailor and a miner, which represent the people who work on the water and on the land. In the center of the seal are four images that represent the state's main industries: agriculture, mining, manufacturing, and navigation. Beneath those images are a cornucopia and a pile of lead, which represent farm products and minerals.

READ ABOUT

A dairy farmer
milks one of
the dairy cows
on his farm in
Wheatland.

CHAPTER EIGHT

ECONOMY

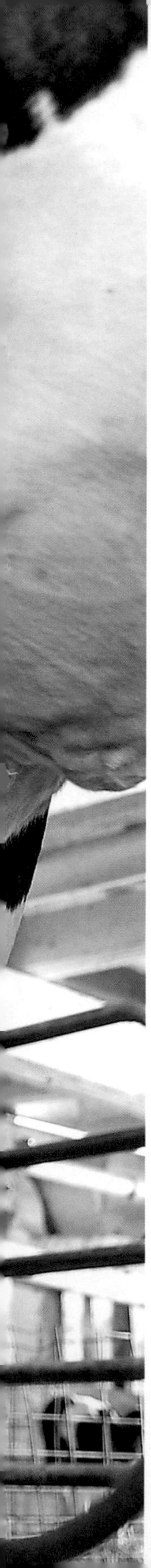

★

WHAT COMES FROM WISCONSIN? The state is a leader in the production of dairy products such as milk and cheese. It also has a strong lumber industry, providing material for building homes and producing paper. But there is more to Wisconsin than just cheese and trees. Wisconsin is second among the states in the percentage of workers involved in manufacturing. In 2012, more than $23 billion in Wisconsin-made goods were shipped to other countries.

Working on a huge vat of cheese at a factory near New Glarus

For decades, Wisconsin dairy farmers fought the sale of margarine, a butter substitute that competed with the sale of real butter. It wasn't legal to buy yellow margarine in Wisconsin until 1967.

CHEESE FOR CHEESEHEADS AND THE REST OF US

There's a reason that Wisconsinites are sometimes nicknamed cheeseheads. The name was meant to be an insult, but many Wisconsinites wear it proudly. In fact, some people wear chunks of foam shaped like wedges of cheddar cheese on their heads at football games.

California surpassed Wisconsin in the number of dairy cattle in 1993, but in 2010 Wisconsin still produced more cheese than the western state.

The United States produces 90 different kinds of cheese. Both Colby (a type of cheddar) and brick (a white cheese) were invented in Wisconsin. Belgian cheese makers brought Limburger to the United States. Only one American cheese maker, located in Monroe, makes the pungent white cheese.

What Do Wisconsinites Do?

This color-coded chart shows what industries Wisconsinites work in.

22.4% Educational services, and health care and social assistance, 639,732

18.6% Manufacturing, 530,612

11.4% Retail trade, 327,344

8.3% Arts, entertainment, and recreation, and accommodation and food services, 237,538

7.8% Professional, scientific, and management, and administrative and waste management services, 223,502

6.3% Finance and insurance, and real estate and rental and leasing, 180,467

5.8% Construction, 165,937

4.6% Transportation and warehousing, and utilities, 130,954

4.1% Other services, except public administration, 116,373

3.5% Public administration, 100,287

2.9% Wholesale trade, 82,578

2.5% Agriculture, forestry, fishing and hunting, and mining, 70,734

1.9% Information, 53,867

Source: U.S. Census Bureau, 2010 census

Top Products

Agriculture Dairy products, corn, cattle and calves, soybeans, potatoes, greenhouse and nursery products

Manufacturing Food and beverages, machinery, fabricated metal products, paper products, chemicals, transportation equipment

Mining Sand and gravel, limestone, lime

Major Agricultural and Mining Products

This map shows where Wisconsin's major agricultural and mining products come from. See the milk carton and cheese? That means dairy products are produced there.

Legend:
- Urban area
- Farming
- Forests, some farming
- Swampland, some farming

N W E S

LAKE SUPERIOR

MINNESOTA

Superior

MICHIGAN

Flambeau

Menominee

Rhinelander

Green Bay

Wausau

Eau Claire

St. Croix

Mississippi

Appleton

Green Bay

Lake Winnebago

La Crosse

Wisconsin

LAKE MICHIGAN

Madison

Milwaukee

Racine

IOWA

ILLINOIS

0   40 Miles
0   40 Kilometers

Key:
- Cattle
- Cranberries
- Dairy
- Fish
- Forest products
- Fruit
- Grains
- Hay
- Hogs
- Lead
- Mineral mining
- Oats
- Potatoes
- Poultry
- Sheep
- Soybeans
- Tobacco
- Vegetables

LUMBER AND PAPER

Although today's forests are not as old or as big as they once were, there is plenty of forestland in Wisconsin. Seventeen million acres (6.9 million ha), or 49 percent of Wisconsin, is still covered with trees. When paper and timber companies cut down trees, they replace them with seedlings.

Strong forests help to make Wisconsin the largest manufacturer of paper in the country—everything from tissue to newsprint to fine letter paper. Kimberly-Clark, the world's largest maker of personal paper products, including Kleenex tissues, was founded at Neenah in 1872.

A VARIETY OF CROPS

Wisconsin leads the nation in growing cranberries, beets for canning, cabbage for sauerkraut, green beans for canning or freezing, and oats. It's also a leader in producing corn for animal feed. The corn is

Wisconsin trees help make the state a leader in paper production.

WORDS TO KNOW

ferments *breaks down*

bogs *marshy lands*

Harvesting cranberries in a
Wisconsin bog

cut, chopped, and stored in silos, where it **ferments**, making a nutritious feed for the state's dairy cattle.

Cranberries are native to Wisconsin's **bogs**. Native Americans used them to make a red dye and also as a salve to draw poisons out of wounds. Today, Wisconsin farmers flood sandy land, primarily around the town of Warrens, to create artificial bogs. About 20,000 acres (8,000 ha) of Wisconsin marshes are used for growing cranberries, making the state the nation's largest producer. In 2012, the state produced more cranberries than the next four states combined.

For hundreds of years, American farmers have exported a root called ginseng to China , where is is used in medicines and nutritional supplements, because it grows more abundantly here than there. Today, several specialized farms in Marathon County produce most of the ginseng root grown in the United States. It takes five years to produce a crop of this herb.

The Ojibwe and Menominee peoples have harvested Wisconsin's wild rice for centuries, but now it's an important crop enjoyed by people all over. The Native Americans have the right to harvest all the wild rice they find in the state, but other people must have licenses to harvest wild rice in Wisconsin.

Wisconsin boasts the largest cooperative of organic farmers in the nation, Organic Valley. Based in La Farge, the group includes about 1,700 farmers in more than 30 states who produce and distribute vegetables, dairy products, and meats.

SCIENTISTS AND INVENTORS

Researchers at the University of Wisconsin–Madison, led by James Thomson, developed a way to grow embryonic stem cells in 1998. Embryonic stem cells are cells that, in the early stages of embryo development, have not yet changed into the cells of the special organs they will become. Stem cells can turn into almost any kind of tissue. Scientists hope they can be specially grown in laboratories and used to treat serious diseases that have no other means of being cured.

Did you know all the letters in the word "typewriter" can be found on the top line of the keyboard? Christopher Sholes of Milwaukee invented the first practical typewriter, a machine for printing words on paper.

NOTABLE WISCONSIN INVENTORS

WHEN?	WHO?	WHERE?	WHAT?
1847	Jerome Case	Racine	Thresher (a machine to separate grain from chaff)
1860	Van Brunt brothers	Mayville	Planter (a machine to both scatter and bury seeds)
1867	Christopher Sholes	Milwaukee	First practical typewriter
1870	Zalmon Simmons	Kenosha	Bedsprings made by machine
1873	J. W. Carhart	Racine	Steam-driven horseless carriage
1878	John Appleby	Mazomanie	Combine (a machine to both thresh and bind wheat)
1883	Warren Johnson	Whitewater	Electric thermostat
1890	Stephen Babcock	Madison	Device to test butterfat content of milk
1890s	Peter Houston	Cambria	Camera tripod
1947	John Bardeen	Madison	Transistor
1952	Les Paul	Waukesha	Solid-body electric guitar

MINI-BIO

JOHN BARDEEN: NOBEL PRIZE WINNER

Not many inventors change the way things work. John Bardeen (1908–1991) of Madison and his colleagues did, when they invented the transistor. Some call it the most important invention of the 20th century. The tiny, cheap transistor sends electricity through a material called a semiconductor. It replaced the large, bulky, and expensive tubes used by devices such as radios, televisions, and computers. He shared the 1956 Nobel Prize in Physics, a feat that he repeated in 1972 for developing a theory of superconductivity—the ability of electricity to flow without resistance through certain materials. Educated at the University of Wisconsin, he's the only scientist ever to win two Nobel Prizes in physics.

? Want to know more? Visit www.factsfornow .scholastic.com and enter the keyword **Wisconsin**.

THE SINKING OF THE *EDMUND FITZGERALD*

The ore freighter *Edmund Fitzgerald* sailed from Superior, Wisconsin, on November 10, 1975. A fierce winter storm sank the ship, killing 29 men. Its story became a popular song by Gordon Lightfoot, "The Wreck of the Edmund Fitzgerald."

Scientists hope that the cells can be developed to become, for example, healthy muscle cells. These cells then could be injected into the body where they would replace diseased cells. Cures might be found for childhood diabetes, Parkinson's, spinal cord injury, and even burns. The university is still leading the way in such research.

SHIPPING AND SHIPBUILDING

New ships were launched at Manitowoc, on Lake Michigan, as early as 1847, when the town made wooden sailing vessels. Even today, it makes luxury yachts, and its high school's sports teams are called the Ships.

The shipping industry began on the Great Lakes in the mid-1800s. Iron ore, wheat, and coal were the main items being transported. By the late 1800s, the lakes were crowded with huge ships carrying cargo. In 1959, the St. Lawrence Seaway opened, bringing international shipping to Lake Superior. Ships from Superior travel through canals to the St. Lawrence River, which feeds into the Atlantic Ocean. Today, goods are also transported in other ways, so ships don't do all of the work. But ships from the United States and Canada still carry cargo across the Great Lakes on a regular basis.

TAKING A CHANCE

In 1988, the federal courts ruled that Native Americans had the right to run gambling casinos, and that states and Indian groups should agree on how this would work. Part of the profit would go to the state, but the Native people themselves would be able to use most of the profits to improve their reservations.

By 2003, all 11 reservations in the state had agreements with Wisconsin. In 2013, the 11 tribes ran 24 casinos throughout the state. In most cases, casino gambling has had a positive impact on Wisconsin's tribal members. The Oneidas, for example, have successfully used earnings from their casinos to improve the economic and social standing of it members. The state has also benefited from Native American-run casinos. From 2000 to 2010, Indian tribes gave the state $576.4 million of the total profits their casinos earned.

Native American industry has led to improvements, such as new schools, on many reservations.

LISTEN FOR THE *VROOM*

Speed and automobile engines fascinated William S. Harley and Arthur Davidson, two young Milwaukee men. The two friends built and sold their first motorcycle in 1903 and continued to improve on their popular machines regularly. By 1911, they were building them with an engine in which the cylinders are mounted in a V shape—giving Harley-Davidson motorcycles their familiar sound. Harleys have been called "hogs" since a Harley racing team had a pig as a mascot. Hundreds of thousands of Harley-Davidson riders drive their bikes to Milwaukee for anniversary events.

At the state's Harley-Davidson motorcycle factory, a worker prepares a V twin engine for shipment.

GETTING AROUND

The oldest road in Wisconsin is Green Bay Road, which goes from the Illinois state line to Green Bay. Originally an Indian trail, it became the main overland route into the state and is now a paved highway through major cities. In 1918, Wisconsin became the first state in the country to give numbers to its major roads.

Wisconsin's primary airport is General Mitchell International Airport in Milwaukee. It's named for Milwaukee-raised U.S. Army general William "Billy" Mitchell, who is recognized as the founder of military aviation in the United States.

MACHINERY

Some of the biggest machines ever made came from Bucyrus International in Milwaukee. Bucyrus machines dug the Panama Canal, and now they are digging the tar sands of Canada for crude oil.

ENERGY FOR THE FUTURE

A dam built on the Fox River at Appleton was the world's first dam to use the power of water to create electricity. That was in 1882, after a paper company executive had learned about Thomas Edison's experiments in producing electricity.

Point Beach Nuclear Power Plant on the Lake Michigan shore near Two Rivers is Wisconsin's only nuclear power plant.

Wind power is growing in Wisconsin. Dozens of large wind turbines are being built in the eastern part of the state that will provide enough power for 15,000 homes. A large wind farm in Dodgeville in the southern part of Wisconsin generates enough power for about 9,000 homes alone.

General William "Billy" Mitchell

LAKE SUPERIOR

Superior
Bayfield
La Pointe
Ashland
Solon Springs
Hurley

MICHIGAN

Hayward
Park Falls
Lac du Flambeau
Grantsburg
Couderay
Minocqua
Eagle River
St. Germain
Rice Lake
Rhinelander
Cameron
Flambeau
St. Croix Falls

Menominee

Egg Harbor
Ephraim

Hudson
Menomonie
Chippewa Falls
Merrill
Antigo
Marinette
Peshtigo

St. Croix

River Falls
Prescott
Eau Claire
Geographic Center of Wisconsin
Wausau
Keshena
Abrams
Green Bay
Sturgeon Bay

Augusta
Stevens Point
Howard
Oneida
Green Bay
Allouez

Marshfield
Ashwaubenon
De Pere
Appleton

Wisconsin Rapids
Plover
Menasha
Kaukauna

Door County

Black River Falls
Nekoosa
Neenah
Two Rivers

MINNESOTA
Wisconsin
Wautoma
Lake Winnebago
Manitowoc

Fountain City
Onalaska
Sparta
Tomah
Oshkosh
Westfield
Ripon
Sheboygan

Camp Douglas
La Crosse
Elroy
Fond du Lac

Mississippi

Wisconsin Dells
Portage
Waupun
West Bend

Baraboo
Beaver Dam
Horicon
Port Washington

Richland Center
Prairie du Sac
Sun Prairie
Hartford
Watertown
Oconomowoc
Wauwatosa

Boscobel
Spring Green
Madison
Lake Mills
Waukesha
Milwaukee
West Allis

Prairie du Chien
Mt. Horeb
Fitchburg
Fort Atkinson

Dodgeville
Stoughton
Whitewater
Racine

Mineral Point
New Glarus
Milton
Delavan

IOWA
Platteville
Belmont
Janesville
Lake Geneva
Kenosha

Monroe
Beloit
Pleasant Prairie

ILLINOIS

LAKE MICHIGAN

Green Bay

N
W E
S

0 _____ 40 Miles
0 _____ 40 Kilometers

90 — Interstate highway

CHAPTER NINE

TRAVEL GUIDE

TRAVEL GUIDE

★

THE SCENERY IN WISCONSIN IS VARIED AND BEAUTIFUL, AND THE STATE PROVIDES LOTS OF TRAILS FOR SEEING IT UP CLOSE. You can also visit museums and historic places to see how this state developed. And if you want pure fun, there is plenty of that, too. So grab a map and a comfortable chair, let your imagination go, and tour Wisconsin!

← Follow along with this travel map. We'll begin in Superior and travel all the way down to Kenosha!

NORTHERN WISCONSIN

THINGS TO DO: Enjoy shimmering lakes and cascading streams, or hike through lush forests.

Superior

★ **Harbor View Park:** Take in the great view at this waterside park on the south shore of Lake Superior.

★ **S.S. *Meteor* Whaleback Ship Museum:** Check out the S.S. *Meteor*, a ship that dates to 1896. Located on Lake Superior's Barker's Island, this museum offers tours of the pilot house, the captain's quarters, and the engine room.

Hayward

★ **National Fresh Water Fishing Hall of Fame:** Take a look at the mounts and photos of record-size fish in this four-story building shaped like a muskellunge fish.

National Fresh Water Fishing Hall of Fame

Lac du Flambeau

★ **Indian Bowl Pow Wows:** Watch or participate in Ojibwe dances and rituals at these pow wows, which take place weekly each summer.

St. Germain

★ **Snowmobile Hall of Fame and Museum:** Here you'll find historic racing snowmobiles, uniforms, trophies, and exhibits related to snowmobiling legends.

Rhinelander Logging Museum

Rhinelander

★ **Rhinelander Logging Museum Complex:** Tour this full-scale reproduction of a 19th-century logging complex.

CENTRAL WISCONSIN

THINGS TO DO: Visit friendly communities along the Mississippi River, tour museums, or watch the Packers in action.

Sailboats in Door County

Kinnickinnic State Park

Sister Bay

★ **Sail Door County:** Climb aboard a sloop, and catch a view of shoreline bluffs, water wildlife, and maybe even a spectacular sunset.

Hudson

★ **Octagon House and the Historic District:** This eight-sided house was built in 1855 and was home to John Moffatt, a local judge. It displays artifacts and antiques from the 19th century.

River Falls

★ **Kinnickinnic State Park:** This 1,242-acre (503 ha) state park features a 70-acre (28 ha) sand delta in the St. Croix River. It's a great place for hiking, boating, or fishing.

Eau Claire

★ **Chippewa Valley Museum:** This award-winning regional museum includes the Anderson Log House and the one-room Sunnyview School.

Augusta

★ **Dells Mill and Museum:** Take a tour of this historic five-story, water-powered gristmill.

SEE IT HERE!
LEGACY CHOCOLATES

Do you love chocolate? Then stop in at Legacy Chocolates in Menomonie. There you can try the mint, the caramel pecan, or the chocolate-on-chocolate truffle. These hand-dipped treats have been featured in national magazines—and you'll see why.

Menomonie

★ **Russell J. Rassbach Heritage Museum:** The displays and artifacts in this museum detail the history of the Dunn County area.

Chippewa Falls

★ **Chippewa Falls Museum of Industry and Technology:** Exhibits here detail the history of the supercomputer and interactive technology.

La Crosse

★ **Children's Museum of La Crosse:** Explore three floors of interactive exhibits and fun at this museum. See a model of a human heart, learn how firefighters save lives, and experiment with light and shadows.

Fond du Lac

★ **Lakeside Park and Lighthouse:** This park has more than 400 acres (160 ha) of recreational space at the south end of Lake Winnebago. You can take a ride on a carousel, a miniature train, and bumper boats. Or just enjoy the view from the top of the lighthouse.

Green Bay

★ **Lambeau Field:** Tour the home of the Green Bay Packers, or bundle up with a winter coat and a blanket and take in a game at this historic stadium.

★ **Green Bay Packer Hall of Fame:** Find out what the Green Bay Packer legend is all about. This museum is a shrine to former Green Bay stars.

Green Bay Packer Hall of Fame

★ **National Railroad Museum:** Here you'll find the nation's oldest and largest railroad museum featuring railroad history and antique trains.

Two Rivers

★ **Historic Rogers Street Fishing Village:** Be sure to see the historic lighthouse, built in 1886, and tour the French Canadian fishing village.

Manitowoc

★ **Wisconsin Maritime Museum:** Check out a collection of model ships and boats, an operating steam engine at this museum, and exhibits of historic vessels. Be sure to take a tour of the USS *Cobia*, a World War II submarine on site.

SOUTHERN WISCONSIN

THINGS TO DO: Enjoy the excitement of Milwaukee, the historic sites of Madison, lake resorts in Lake Geneva, or miles of entertainment and water park fun in Wisconsin Dells.

Madison

★ **Wisconsin Historical Museum:** Wisconsin's main historical museum, this is the place to see both permanent and rotating exhibits presented by the Wisconsin State Historical Society.

★ **Wisconsin State Capitol:** Take a guided tour through the hallways of the recently refurbished capitol. See the legislative chambers, where Wisconsin lawmakers make some of the state's most important decisions.

Viewing the Declaration of Independence on display at the Wisconsin capitol

★ **University of Wisconsin Geology Museum:** Check out a wide variety of exhibits on the geological history of Wisconsin, from minerals to fossils to dinosaur bones.

★ **Little Amerricka Amusement Park at Marshall:** Featuring three small roller coasters, bumper cars, a Ferris wheel, and narrow gauge steam and diesel locomotives, this is one amusement park that is a blast.

Mineral Point

★ **Pendarvis:** This site preserves stone cottages built by early 19th-century immigrants from Cornwall, in southwestern England, and interprets the history of Cornish settlement and Wisconsin's lead-mining heyday. Try a pasty or other authentic Cornish fare at the internationally recognized Pendarvis House Restaurant.

Spring Green

★ **Taliesin:** This is the most notable of all the Frank Lloyd Wright buildings in Wisconsin. Made of limestone, wood, and glass to mirror its natural setting, this home and studio complex is regarded as the architect's "self-portrait" and offers a glimpse at many of his experimental styles. The house features furniture he designed.

Garden statue at the House on the Rock

THE HOUSE ON THE ROCK

When you walk into the House on the Rock, Wisconsin's most popular tourist attraction, you're not quite sure what you're seeing. The stone house Alex Jordan built on top of a column of rock near the Wisconsin River between Spring Green and Dodgeville became 16 buildings that house amazing collections of all kinds. Some items are genuine historical artifacts, some are fakes—but no one knows which are which. It also holds the world's largest carousel, with 175 wooden animals. A cantilevered room, or a room with apparently no support under it, stretches out 218 feet (66 m) over the valley. Those who aren't afraid of heights can look out any of the 3,264 windows to the ground 156 feet (48 m) below.

SEE IT HERE!
THE ICE AGE NATIONAL SCENIC TRAIL

The last ice age is called the Wisconsin because you can see more of its effects in Wisconsin than anywhere else. The Ice Age National Scenic Trail meanders for 1,200 miles (1,900 km) through Wisconsin. The trail follows the edge of the last glaciers. You can walk it or drive it. One of the best ways to start to understand the drumlins, kames, kettles, and moraines you're seeing is to stop at the Ice Age Visitors Center at Kettle Moraine North State Forest headquarters near Milwaukee. They'll set you off in the right direction to explore the state's amazing geology.

Milwaukee

★ **Milwaukee Public Museum:** This natural and human history museum features many permanent and special exhibits, from animal habitats to ancient temples and tombs to mummies.

★ **Milwaukee Art Museum:** The building itself is a work of art, complete with a 90-foot (27-m) glass-walled reception hall right on Lake Michigan. Visitors will see a wide variety of exhibits, from contemporary art and photography to African art and a Haitian collection.

SEE IT HERE!
SUMMERFEST

The state's largest festival, called Summerfest, is held along the lakefront in Milwaukee. Begun in the 1960s, it may be the world's largest music festival. It lasts 11 days each summer, filling 10 different stages plus an auditorium with a great variety of music from morning to night. Around a million people enjoy Summerfest each year.

The Milwaukee Mile speed track in West Allis opened in 1903, eight years before the famous Indianapolis Motor Speedway, home of the Indy 500.

★ **International Clown Hall of Fame and Research Center:** Featuring memorabilia and various exhibits on the history of clowning, this museum honors some of the world's top clowns.

★ **Discovery World Center for Public Innovation:** With more than 140 interactive exhibits, this museum should capture the curiosity of visitors both young and old.

★ **Miller Park:** At this ballpark, you can cheer for the Milwaukee Brewers as they take on their rivals in the National League Central Division.

★ **Milwaukee County Zoo:** This zoo features more than 2,500 animals, including king penguins, Chinese alligators, leopard sharks, and red pandas.

Rhinoceros horrbills at the Milwaukee County Zoo

West Allis

★ **Wisconsin State Fair:** At the state fair, you can check out exhibits of agriculture and crafts, go on fun rides, and enjoy some famous Wisconsin cheese.

The Wisconsin State Fair

Lake Geneva

★ **Lake Geneva:** Go waterskiing, tubing, and camping along this beautiful, crystal-clear lake, or explore historic Yerkes Observatory.

Watertown

★ **Octagon House:** This eight-sided house was built in 1854 by John Richards, a pioneer Watertown settler. A historic five-story, 57-room pre–Civil War home, it housed the first kindergarten in America.

Octagon House

Wisconsin Dells

★ **Mt. Olympus Water and Theme Park:** This water and theme park features outdoor roller coasters, go-karts, waterslides, and lazy rivers.

★ **Noah's Ark Waterpark:** Ride the thrilling waterslides and waves at America's largest water park.

★ **Tommy Bartlett's Exploratory:** With more than 100 science and technology exhibits, plus an original Russian *Mir* Space Station, this is a must-see attraction.

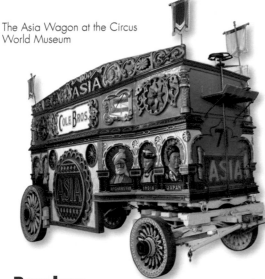

The Asia Wagon at the Circus World Museum

Baraboo

★ **Circus World Museum:** Housed on the grounds of the original Ringling Bros. and Barnum & Bailey Circus winter quarters, the museum holds the world's largest collection of historic circus wagons.

Pleasant Prairie

★ **Jelly Belly Visitor Center:** Check out the warehouse of the Jelly Belly jelly bean. Take a tour of the warehouse and learn about the company's jelly beans, taffy, candy corn, gummies, and more.

Touring the Jelly Belly factory

Kenosha

★ **Dinosaur Discovery Museum:** Learn about the links between ancient dinosaurs and modern-day birds at this museum. Also check out dinosaur bones, life-size replicas, and interactive exhibits.

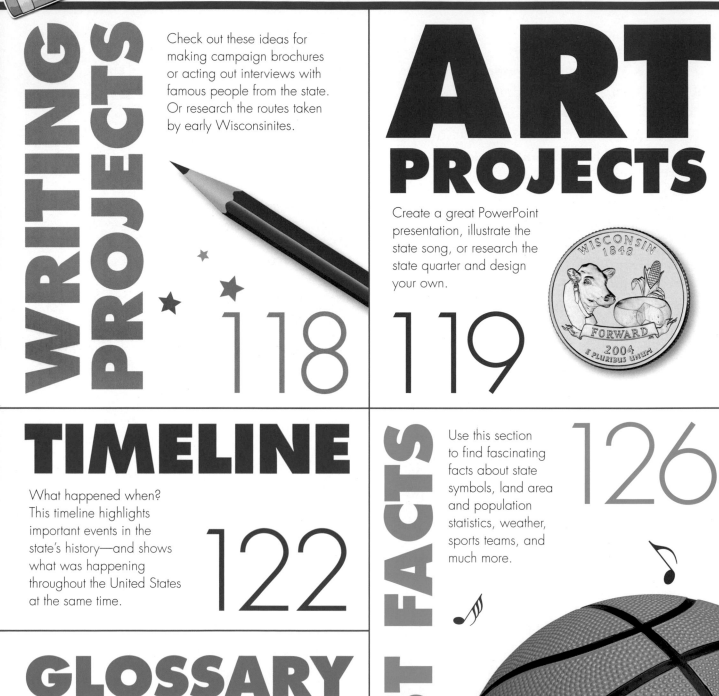

WRITING PROJECTS

Check out these ideas for making campaign brochures or acting out interviews with famous people from the state. Or research the routes taken by early Wisconsinites.

118

ART PROJECTS

Create a great PowerPoint presentation, illustrate the state song, or research the state quarter and design your own.

119

WISCONSIN
1848
FORWARD
2004
E PLURIBUS UNUM

TIMELINE

What happened when? This timeline highlights important events in the state's history—and shows what was happening throughout the United States at the same time.

122

FAST FACTS

Use this section to find fascinating facts about state symbols, land area and population statistics, weather, sports teams, and much more.

126

GLOSSARY

Remember the Words to Know from the chapters in this book? They're all collected here.

125

SCIENCE, TECHNOLOGY, ENGINEERING, & MATH PROJECTS

120

Make weather maps, graph population statistics, and research endangered species that live in the state.

PRIMARY VS. SECONDARY SOURCES

121

So what are primary and secondary sources, and what's the diff? This section explains all that and where you can find them.

BIOGRAPHICAL DICTIONARY

133

This at-a-glance guide highlights some of the state's most important and influential people. Visit this section to read about their contributions to the state, the country, and the world.

RESOURCES

Books and much more. Take a look at these additional sources for information about the state.

138

WRITING PROJECTS

Create an Election Brochure or Web Site!

Run for office!

Throughout this book, you've read about some of the issues that concern Wisconsin today. As a candidate for governor of Wisconsin, create a campaign brochure or Web site. Explain how you meet the qualifications to be governor, and talk about the three or four major issues you'll focus on if you're elected. Remember, you'll be responsible for Wisconsin's budget. How would you spend the taxpayers' money?

SEE: Chapter Seven, page 86–87.

Compare and Contrast— When, Why, and How Did They Come?

Compare the migration and explorations of Wisconsin's Native people and its first European explorers. Tell about:

★ When their migrations began

★ How they traveled

★ Why they migrated

★ Where their journeys began and ended

★ What they found when they arrived

    SEE: Chapters Two and Three, pages 22–39.

Conduct an Interview with an Important Wisconsinite

Gather up a pen, a notepad, a voice recorder, and a friend. Look at biographies (books about people by other people), autobiographies and memoirs (books people have written about themselves), and online to see what you can find out about some of the people you have learned about in this book, including Frank Lloyd Wright, Golda Meir, Gaylord Nelson, Hank Aaron, Brett Favre, Les Paul, and many more. Be sure to use at least three sources. Then, with a friend, write and perform an interview of that person on a voice recorder and present it to your class.

SEE: Chapter Six and the Biographical Dictionary, pages 76–79, 133–136.

Hank Aaron

ART PROJECTS

Create a PowerPoint Presentation or Visitors' Guide

Welcome to Wisconsin!

Wisconsin's a great place to visit and to live. From its natural beauty to its bustling cities and historic sites, there's plenty to see and do. In your PowerPoint presentation or brochure, highlight 10 to 15 of Wisconsin's amazing landmarks. Be sure to include:

★ a map of the state showing where these sites are located

★ photos, illustrations, Web links, natural history facts, geographic stats, climate and weather, and plants and wildlife.

SEE: Chapter One, pages 9–21 and Chapter Nine, pages 106–115.

Illustrate the Lyrics to the Wisconsin State Song ("On, Wisconsin")

Use markers, paints, photos, collage, colored pencils, or computer graphics to illustrate the lyrics to "On, Wisconsin," the state song. Turn your illustrations into a picture book, or scan them into a PowerPoint presentation and add music.

SEE: The lyrics to "On, Wisconsin" on page 128.

State Quarter Project

From 1999 to 2008, the U.S. Mint introduced new quarters commemorating each of the 50 states in the order that they were admitted to the Union. Each state's quarter features a unique design on its back, or reverse.

★ Go to www.factsfornow.scholastic.com and enter the keyword **Wisconsin**. Look for the link for the Wisconsin quarter to find out what's featured onthe back. (Here's a hint: the state's economy played a big part in what was chosen for the design!)

★ Research the significance of each image. Who designed the quarter? Who chose the final design?

★ Design your own Wisconsin quarter. What images would you choose for the reverse?

★ Make a poster showing the Wisconsin quarter and label each image.

SCIENCE, TECHNOLOGY, ENGINEERING, & MATH PROJECTS

Track Endangered Species

Using your knowledge of Wisconsin's wildlife, research what animals and plants are endangered or threatened.

★ Find out what the state is doing to protect these species.

★ Chart known populations of the animals and plants, and report on changes in certain geographical areas.

SEE: Chapter One, page 21.

Whooping crane

Graph Population Statistics

★ Compare population statistics (such as ethnic background, birth, death, and literacy rates) in Wisconsin counties or major cities.

★ In your graph or chart, look at population density, and write sentences describing what the population statistics show; graph one set of population statistics, and write a paragraph explaining what the graphs reveal.

SEE: Chapter Six, pages 68–72.

Create a Weather Map of Wisconsin

Use your knowledge of Wisconsin's geography to research and identify conditions that result in specific weather events, including thunderstorms and tornadoes. What is it about the climate of Wisconsin that makes it vulnerable to things such as tornadoes? Create a weather map or poster showing the weather patterns over the state in different seasons. Include a caption explaining the technology used to measure weather phenomena such as tornadoes and provide data.

SEE: Chapter One, page 17.

PRIMARY VS. SECONDARY SOURCES

What's the Diff?

Your teacher may require at least one or two primary sources and one or two secondary sources for your assignment. So, what's the difference between the two?

★ **Primary sources are original.** You are reading the actual words of someone's diary, journal, letter, autobiography, or interview. Primary sources can also be photographs, maps, prints, cartoons, news/film footage, posters, first-person newspaper articles, drawings, musical scores, and recordings. By the way, when you conduct a survey, interview someone, shoot a video, or take photographs to include in a project, you are creating primary sources!

★ **Secondary sources are what you find in encyclopedias, textbooks, articles, biographies, and almanacs.** These are written by a person or group of people who tell about something that happened to someone else. Secondary sources also recount what another person said or did. This book is an example of a secondary source.

Now that you know what primary sources are—where can you find them?

★ **Your school or local library:** Check the library catalog for collections of original writings, government documents, musical scores, and so on. Some of this material may be stored on microfilm.

★ **Historical societies:** These organizations keep historical documents, photographs, and other materials. Staff members can help you find what you are looking for. History museums are also great places to see primary sources firsthand.

★ **The Internet:** There are lots of sites that have primary sources you can download and use in a project or assignment.

TIMELINE

★ ★ ★

U.S. Events `1600` Wisconsin Events

Jean Nicolet coming ashore

1634
Jean Nicolet becomes the first European to reach Wisconsin.

1661
Ménard and Groseilliers travel up the Fox River to the Wisconsin and down to the Mississippi.

1669
A Catholic mission is established at Green Bay.

1682
René-Robert Cavelier, Sieur de La Salle, claims more than 1 million square miles (2.6 million sq km) of territory in the Mississippi River basin for France, naming it Louisiana.

1685
A permanent settlement at Prairie du Chien on the Mississippi becomes important trading post.

`1700`

1743
Lead mining begins in Wisconsin.

1763
Great Britain gains control of Wisconsin from the French.

1776
Thirteen American colonies declare their independence from Great Britain, marking the beginning of the Revolutionary War.

1783
Wisconsin becomes United States territory.

1787
The U.S. Constitution is written.

`1800`

1812–15
The United States and Great Britain fight the War of 1812.

1832
The Black Hawk War ends Native American resistance to white settlers.

1836
Wisconsin Territory is established.

U.S. Events

Wisconsin Events

1837
The Ojibwe sign a treaty giving up their land titles but keeping the right to hunt and fish on the ceded territory.

1846–48
The United States fights a war with Mexico over western territories in the Mexican War.

1846
Three settlements are merged into the city of Milwaukee.

1848
Wisconsin becomes the 30th state.

1861–65
The American Civil War is fought between the Northern Union and the Southern Confederacy; it ends with the surrender of the Confederate army, led by General Robert E. Lee.

1866
Wisconsin's African Americans are given the right to vote.

1871
The Peshtigo fire kills at least 2,400 people.

1886
Apache leader Geronimo surrenders to the U.S. Army, ending the last major Native American rebellion against the expansion of the United States into the West.

1900

1900
Robert M. La Follette is elected governor and brings reforms.

1910
Victor Berger of Milwaukee becomes the first Socialist elected to Congress.

1917–18
The United States is involved in World War I.

1920
The Nineteenth Amendment to the U.S. Constitution grants women the right to vote.

1929
The stock market crashes, plunging the United States deeper into the Great Depression.

1932
Wisconsin enacts the nation's first unemployment compensation law.

1941–45
The United States engages in World War II.

1946
German and Japanese prisoners of war leave Wisconsin.

1950–53
The United States engages in the Korean War.

U.S. Events

1954

The U.S. Supreme Court prohibits segregation of public schools in the *Brown v. Board of Education* ruling.

1964–73

The United States engages in the Vietnam War.

A protest over segregated schools

1991

The United States and other nations fight the brief Persian Gulf War against Iraq.

2001

Terrorists hijack four U.S. aircraft and crash them into the World Trade Center in New York City, the Pentagon in Washington, D.C., and a Pennsylvania field, killing thousands.

2003

The United States and coalition forces invade Iraq.

Wisconsin Events

1954

The U.S. Senate censures Senator Joseph McCarthy.

1959

The St. Lawrence Seaway opens, bringing international shipping to Wisconsin ports.

1975

The Menominee Nation regains federal recognition.

1979

Milwaukee is forced to start desegregating schools.

1997

Wisconsin Works program is enacted.

1998

The U.S. Supreme Court allows Wisconsin's educational voucher plan to include private religious schools.

2000

2003

All 11 Native American groups in Wisconsin have agreements to operate gambling establishments on Indian lands.

2012

Two unrelated shootings in Oak Creek and Brookfield leave several people dead.

GLOSSARY

★　　★　　★

archaeologists scientists who study the remains of cultures

bogs marshy lands

communism a system in which all property and goods are owned by everyone and controlled by the government

deciduous types of trees that lose their leaves each year

developers people who change natural areas into land used for houses or businesses

effigy a figure of a person or animal

erosion the process of land being worn away by wind, water, or other factors

ferments breaks down

flowage a lake created when a dam backs up the water in a river

fugitive a person hiding from other people

glaciers slow-moving bodies of ice

irrigation watering land by artificial means to promote plant growth

mollusks shellfish

saplings young trees

segregated separated from another group, usually by race or gender

shaman a priest who cures people and communicates with the spirit world for the group

FAST FACTS

★ ★ ★

State Symbols

Statehood date	May 29, 1848, the 30th state
Origin of state name	A Miami Indian word believed to mean "river that meanders through something red"
State capital	Madison
State nickname	Badger State
State motto	"Forward"
State bird	Robin
State flower	Wood violet
State fish	Muskellunge
State stone	Red granite
State song	"On, Wisconsin" (see page 128 for lyrics)
State tree	Sugar maple
State fair	West Allis (early August)

State seal

Geography

Total area; rank	65,498 square miles (169,640 sq km); 23rd
Land; rank	54,310 square miles (140,663 sq km); 25th
Water; rank	11,188 square miles (28,977 sq km); 4th
Inland water; rank	1,830 square miles (4,740 sq km); 11th
Great Lakes; rank	9,358 square miles (24,237 sq km); 2nd
Geographic center	Wood County, 9 miles (14.5 km) southeast of Marshfield
Latitude	42° 30' N to 47° 3' N
Longitude	86° 49' W to 92° 54' W
Highest point	Timm's Hill, 1,952 feet (595 m)
Lowest point	579 feet (176 m) along Lake Michigan
Largest city	Milwaukee
Number of counties	72
Longest river	Wisconsin River, 430 miles (692 km)

State flag

Population

Population; rank (2010 census): 5,586,986; 20th
Density (2010 census): 105 persons per square mile (41 per sq km)
Population distribution (2010 census): 70% urban, 30% rural
Race (2010 census): White persons: 83.3%

Black persons: 6.2%

Asian persons: 2.3%

American Indian and Alaska Native persons: 0.9%

Persons reporting two or more races: 1.4%

Hispanic or Latino persons: 5.9%

People of some other race: 0.1%

Weather

Record high temperature 114°F (46°C) at Wisconsin Dells on July 13, 1936
Record low temperature −55°F (−48°C) at Couderay on February 4, 1996
Average July temperature, Milwaukee 72°F (22°C)
Average January temperature, Milwaukee 22°F (−6°C)
Average yearly precipitation, Milwaukee 34.8 in. (88.4 cm)

Ice fishing on a cold day

STATE SONG

★ ★ ★

"On, Wisconsin"

William T. Purdy wrote the music for the state song in 1909. Originally written as a fight song for the University of Wisconsin, the words were altered in 1959, when the song was adopted as the state song.

On, Wisconsin. On, Wisconsin.
Grand old badger state.
We, thy loyal sons and daughters,
Hail thee, good and great.
On, Wisconsin. On, Wisconsin.
Champion of the right,
"Forward," our motto—
God will give thee might.

NATURAL AREAS AND HISTORIC SITES

★ ★ ★

National Lakeshores and Riverways

Apostle Islands National Lakeshore comprises islands and the Bayfield Peninsula on Lake Superior.

St. Croix National Scenic Riverway contains 252 miles (406 km) of the St. Croix and Namekagon Rivers.

National Scenic Trails

The *North Country National Scenic Trail* crosses part of Wisconsin and the *Ice Age National Scenic Trail* lies entirely within Wisconsin. The latter skirts glacial lakebeds, drumlins, and moraines, among other remains from the Wisconsin ice age.

National Forests

Chequamegon National Forest is Wisconsin's largest national forest.

Nicolet National Forest, in northeastern Wisconsin, has more than 260 lakes.

State Parks and Forests

About one-seventh of all Wisconsin's land is state or national parks and forests. Wisconsin has 14 state forests, 50 state parks, 42 state trails, and eight recreation areas. The largest state forest, *North Highland–American Legion State Forest*, covers more than 225,000 acres (91,000 ha) in northern Wisconsin. The largest state park is Devil's Lake.

A kayaker on Lake Superior explores the sea caves on Devil's Island.

SPORTS TEAMS

★ ★ ★

NCAA Teams (Division I)

Marquette University *Golden Eagles*
University of Wisconsin–Green Bay *Phoenix*
University of Wisconsin–Madison *Badgers*
University of Wisconsin–Milwaukee *Panthers*

PROFESSIONAL SPORTS TEAMS

★ ★ ★

Major League Baseball
Milwaukee *Brewers*

National Basketball Association
Milwaukee *Bucks*

National Football League
Green Bay *Packers*

CULTURAL INSTITUTIONS

Libraries

The *Milwaukee Public Library* is the leading public library in the state.

The *Wisconsin State Historical Society Library* (Madison) contains extensive collections on state history and the region.

The *Memorial Library* at University of Wisconsin–Madison houses the largest single library collection in the state.

Museums

The *Chippewa Valley Museum* (Eau Claire) features exhibits about the Ojibwe and the settlement of the valley in northwestern Wisconsin.

The *State Historical Museum* (Madison) contains extensive collections on Wisconsin history.

The *Madison Museum of Contemporary Art* (Madison) has about 5,000 works by artists of the 20th and 21st centuries.

The *Racine Art Museum* features contemporary crafts, including an extensive collection of ceramics, fibers, and glass, metal, and wood objects.

The *Milwaukee Public Museum* is one of the largest natural history museums in the United States.

The *Rhinelander Logging Museum Complex* houses its exhibits in a replica of an old-time logging camp.

The *Experimental Aircraft Association Museum* (Oshkosh) and *National Railroad Museum* (Green Bay) contain fine collections of air and rail equipment.

Performing Arts

The *Florentine Opera Company* (Milwaukee) presents classic and new American operas at the Marcus Center in the city's downtown area.

The *Madison Symphony Orchestra* (Madison) features an enormous organ that is the largest movable object in any theater in the country.

Universities and Colleges

In 2011, Wisconsin had 14 public and 50 private institutions of higher learning.

ANNUAL EVENTS

January–March

World Championship Snowmobile Derby in Eagle River (January)

Hot Air Affair in Hudson (February)

American Birkebeiner in Cable and Hayward (February)

Milwaukee Journal Sentinel Sports Show (March)

April–June

Chocolate Fest in Burlington (May)

Horicon Marsh Bird Festival (May)

Walleye Weekend in Fond du Lac (June)

Summerfest in Milwaukee (June)

July–September

Art Fair on the Square in Madison (July)

Dane County Fair in Madison (July)

Great Circus Parade in Milwaukee (July)

Lumberjack World Championships in Hayward (July)

Wisconsin State Fair in Milwaukee (July)

EAA AirVenture in Oshkosh (July–August)

World Championship Off-Road Races in Crandon (August–September)

Cranberry Festival in Warrens (September)

Oktoberfest in La Crosse (September–October)

Colorama, statewide (September)

October–December

World Dairy Expo in Madison (October)

Holiday Folk Fair in Milwaukee (November)

Christmas in the Air in Oshkosh (December)

Winterfest in Milwaukee (December)

Hot-air balloons in the Wisconsin Dells

Henry "Hank" Aaron See page 79.

Kareem Abdul-Jabar (1947–) is a basketball great. Born Lew Alcindor, he led the Milwaukee Bucks to the NBA championship in 1971.

Waldemar Ager (1869–1941) was an editor, author, and lecturer best known for his work supporting the temperance movement. Born in Norway, Ager spent most of his life in Eau Claire.

Edward P. Allis (1824–1889) was a manufacturer of heavy machinery. Born in New York, Allis moved to Wisconsin in 1846.

Don Ameche (1908–1993) was an actor who won an Academy Award for his role in *Cocoon*. He was born in Kenosha.

Roy Chapman Andrews (1884–1960) was an explorer and museum director who, in 1923 in Mongolia, became the first person to discover dinosaur eggs. He was born in Beloit.

Walter Annenberg (1908–2002) was the founder of *TV Guide* and *Seventeen* magazines. He donated millions of dollars to schools, hospitals, and other causes. He was born in Milwaukee.

John Bardeen See page 102.

H. H. Bennett (1843–1908) was a photographer best known for his pictures of the Wisconsin Dells. He invented a shutter device that allowed photographers to take clear pictures of moving subjects, which became known as stop action.

Victor Berger (1860–1929) was a founder of the National Socialist Party and the first Socialist elected to the U.S. Congress. Born in Austria-Hungary, Berger settled in Milwaukee in 1891.

Jacob Best (1786–1861) founded what would become the Pabst Brewing Company. He was born in Germany but moved to Milwaukee in 1844.

Carrie Jacobs Bond (1862–1946) was a songwriter remembered for "I Love You Truly." She was born in Janesville.

Olympia Brown See page 57.

Chief Buffalo See page 47.

Seymour Cray (1925–1996) was the inventor of the supercomputer. He was born in Chippewa Falls.

Patrick Cudahy (1849–1919) was a businessperson, mainly in the meat-packing industry. Born in Ireland, he lived in Milwaukee and founded the city of Cudahy.

Willem Dafoe (1958–) is a stage and movie actor. One of his roles is of Norman Osborn/ Green Goblin in *Spider-Man*. He was born in Appleton.

Ada E. Deer (1935–) is a Native American activist who helped end the U.S. policy of Indian termination. She was born on the Menominee Reservation.

Michael Dhuey (1958–) is a computer engineer known as the co-inventor of the Mac II computer in 1987 and co-developer of the hardware for the original iPod in 2001. He was born in Milwaukee.

Ada E. Deer

Charles de Langlade See page 35.

Henry Dodge (1782–1867) was a U.S. soldier during the Black Hawk War. He became Wisconsin's first territorial governor and, later, a U.S. senator.

James Doty (1799–1865) was the second governor of Wisconsin Territory. He was born in New York and spent most of his life in Wisconsin, living in Prairie du Chien, Green Bay, and Neenah, among other places.

Ole Evinrude (1877–1934) was the inventor of the outboard motor. He was born in Norway and grew up near Cambridge.

Chris Farley (1964–1997) was a comedian on *Saturday Night Live*. He was born in Madison.

Brett Favre (1969–) was the quarterback of the Green Bay Packers from 1992 to 2007.

Edna Ferber (1885–1968) was a Pulitzer Prize–winning author. She spent her high school and college years in Appleton.

Zona Gale (1874–1938) was a Pulitzer Prize–winning writer. She was born in Portage.

Hamlin Garland (1860–1940) was a Pulitzer Prize–winning autobiographer and novelist. He was born in West Salem.

William Goodell (1792–1878) was a prominent abolitionist and journalist who helped found two antislavery societies in the 1830s. He ran for president in 1852 and 1860 on a platform for the complete abolition of slavery. He was born in New York and died in Janesville in southern Wisconsin.

Augustin Grignon (1780–1860) was a fur trader who operated a store in Green Bay.

Owen Gromme (1896–1991) was a nature artist. He was born in Fond du Lac.

Father James Groppi See page 62.

Gary Gygax (1938–) is the coauthor of the Dungeons & Dragons role-playing game. He lived and started his business in Lake Geneva.

William S. Harley (1880–1943) was coinventor of the Harley-Davidson motorcycle. He and Arthur Davidson built their first motorcycle in 1903 in Milwaukee.

Eric Heiden (1958–) is a speed skater who won five gold medals at the 1980 Winter Olympics. He was born in Madison.

Edna Ferber

Eric Heiden

Marguerite Henry (1902–1997) was a Newbery Award–winning author of books about horses, including *Misty of Chincoteague*. She was born in Milwaukee.

Woody Herman (1913–1987) was a jazz musician and bandleader. He was born Woodrow Charles Herman in Milwaukee.

William Hoard (1836–1918) was governor of Wisconsin and an important contributor to the development of its dairy industry.

James Horlick (1844–1921) and **William Horlick (1846–1936)** were the inventors of malted milk. Born in England, the brothers established their company in Racine.

Harry Houdini (1874–1926) was a famed magician and escape artist. Born in Hungary, he was raised in Appleton.

Orrin Ingram (1830–1918) was a businessperson and inventor. Born in Massachusetts, he settled in Eau Claire and formed the first of many lumber firms.

Samuel Curtis Johnson (1833–1919) was a businessperson. Born in Ohio, he founded S. C. Johnson & Son, one of the world's leading manufacturers of household cleaning products, in Racine.

Solomon Juneau (1793–1856) was a fur trader and politician. He helped to incorporate Milwaukee and served as the city's first mayor.

Frank O. King (1883–1969) was a cartoonist best remembered for the *Gasoline Alley* comic strip. He was born in Cashton.

Pee Wee King (1914–2000) was a singer and an important figure in country music. He was born in Milwaukee.

Robert M. La Follette (1855–1925) was a U.S. congressman, governor of Wisconsin, and a U.S. senator.

E. L. "Curly" Lambeau (1898–1965) was a cofounder of the Green Bay Packers. He also played on and coached the team.

Aldo Leopold (1887–1948) was a founder of the environmental movement. Born in Iowa, he came to know the Madison area when he worked for the Forest Products Laboratory.

Liberace (1919–1987) was a classical pianist and performer. His full name was Wladzlu Valentino Liberace, and he was born in West Allis.

Vince Lombardi (1913–1970) was the Green Bay Packers coach who led the team to two Super Bowl championships. He was born in Brooklyn, New York.

Vince Lombardi

Jim Lovell (1928–) is a former U.S. astronaut, famous as the commander of the *Apollo 13* mission, which suffered mechanical problems on its way to the moon. With the help of Mission Control in Texas, he and his crew safely brought the craft back to Earth.

Jackie Mason (1931–) is a stand-up comedian who often uses his Jewish background for his humor. He was born as Yacov Moshe Maza in Sheboygan.

Joseph McCarthy (1908–1957) was a U.S. senator remembered for Senate hearings on communism.

Helen Farnsworth Mears (1873–1916) was a sculptor. She was born and raised in Oshkosh.

Golda Meir (1898–1978) was a Russian Jewish immigrant who attended school in Milwaukee and became Israeli prime minister in 1969.

Frederick Miller (1824–1888) was a German brewer who immigrated to Milwaukee and founded the Miller Brewing Company, which is still in operation today.

Steve Miller (1943–) is a blues and rock musician and leader of the Steve Miller Band. Some of his hits from the 1970s include "Jungle Love," "Fly Like an Eagle," and "Take the Money and Run." He was born in Milwaukee.

William "Billy" Mitchell (1879–1936) is considered the Father of the U.S. Air Force. He was born in France and grew up in Milwaukee.

John Muir (1838–1914) was a naturalist. He was born in Scotland but raised near Portage. He attended the University of Wisconsin–Madison. He founded the Sierra Club.

Gaylord Nelson See page 19.

Sterling North (1906–1974) was the author of *Rascal* and *Midnight and Jeremiah*. He was born and raised in Edgerton.

Georgia O'Keeffe (1887–1986) was a painter of southwestern scenes. She was born and raised in Sun Prairie.

Georgia O'Keeffe

Frederick Pabst (1836–1904) was an American brewer, born in Germany.

Les Paul (1915–2009) was a jazz guitarist who helped develop the electric guitar. He was born in Waukesha.

Vel Phillips See page 89.

William Rehnquist (1924–2005) was the chief justice of the U.S. Supreme Court from 1986 to 2005. He was born in Milwaukee.

Aaron Rogers (1983–) is a football quarterback playing for the Green Bay Packers. He led his team to the 2010 Super Bowl championship and was named the Most Valuable Player of the game.

Paul Ryan (1970–) was elected a Wisconsin member of the U.S. House of Representatives in 1998. He was the Republican Party nominee for vice president in the 2012 election.

Joseph Schlitz (1831–1875) was a German entrepreneur who came to Milwaukee and assumed control of Krug Brewing Company, which he renamed Schlitz Brewing Company.

Carl Schurz (1829–1906) was a Union army general in the Civil War and secretary of the interior under President Rutherford B. Hayes.

Tony Shalhoub (1953–), born in Green Bay, is an actor known for his roles as Adrian Monk in the TV series *Monk* and as Antonio Scarpacci in *Wings*. He has won three Emmy Awards and a Golden Globe Award for his work.

Donald "Deke" Slayton (1924–1993) was one of original seven Mercury astronauts. He was born in Sparta.

Bart Starr (1934–) was quarterback for the Green Bay Packers from 1956 to 1971. He was born in Alabama.

Harry Steenbock (1886–1967), born in New Holstein, was a professor of biochemistry at the University of Wisconsin. He demonstrated that exposing foods to ultraviolet light increased their vitamin D content. His invention helped eliminate rickets, a disease caused by the body's lack of vitamin D.

Edward Steichen (1879–1973) was a Luxembourg-born photographer. He began his career in Milwaukee.

George Edwin Taylor (1857–1925) was the first African American to run for president of the United States, in 1904. He was born in Arkansas and moved to Wisconsin, where he worked as a journalist and political activist.

Joseph Thorp (1812–1895) was a lumberman, merchant, and politician. Born in New York, he established the Eau Claire Lumber Company.

Spencer Tracy (1900–1967) was an Academy Award–winning actor. He was born in Milwaukee.

Frederick Jackson Turner (1861–1932) was a historian of the American West. He was born and raised in Portage.

Bob Uecker (1935–) played baseball for the Milwaukee Braves and is now a sportscaster. He was born in Milwaukee.

Greta Van Susteren (1954–) is a commentator and TV personality who hosts *On the Record*, a program devoted to politics and current events. She was born in Appleton.

Orson Wells (1915–1985) was a screenwriter and movie director. Many consider his *Citizen Kane* to be the best film of all time. He was born in Kenosha.

Reggie White (1961–2004) was a football player for the Green Bay Packers between 1993 and 1998. He was inducted into the Football Hall of Fame in 2006.

Ella Wheeler Wilcox (1850–1919) was a poet who was born in Johnstown.

Gene Wilder (1933–) is a movie writer, director, and producer. He was born Jerome Silberman in Milwaukee.

Laura Ingalls Wilder See page 43.

Thornton Wilder (1897–1975) was a playwright and novelist. He was born in Madison.

Frances Willard (1839–1889) was the founder of the Women's Christian Temperance Union. She was raised in Janesville.

Oprah Winfrey (1954–) is a talk show host, television performer, and entertainment executive. She was born in Mississippi but spent much of her childhood in Milwaukee.

Frank Lloyd Wright See page 73.

Oprah Winfrey

RESOURCES

★ ★ ★

BOOKS

Nonfiction

Bie, Michael. *It Happened in Wisconsin*. Guilford, Ct.: Globe Pequot, 2013.

Bowes, John P. *Black Hawk and the War of 1832: Removal in the North*. New York: Chelsea House, 2007.

Dwyer, Helen, and Sierra Adare. *Ojibwe History and Culture*. New York: Gareth Stevens, 2012.

Kann, Bob. *Belle and Bob La Follette: Partners in Politics*. Madison, Wis.: Wisconsin Historical Society Press, 2008.

Porter, Adele. *Wild About Wisconsin Birds: A Youth's Guide to the Birds of Wisconsin*. Cambridge, Minn.: Adventure Publications, 2009.

Sports Illustrated. *Sports Illustrated Packers: Green, Gold and Glory*. New York: Time Home Entertainment, 2013.

Fiction

Brink, Carol Ryrie. *Caddie Woodlawn*. New York: The Macmillan Company, 1935.

Enright, Elizabeth. *Thimble Summer*. New York: Holt, Rinehart, and Winston, 1938.

Wilder, Laura Ingalls. *Little House in the Big Woods*. New York: Harper & Brothers, 1932.

Visit this Scholastic Web site for more information on Wisconsin:
www.factsfornow.scholastic.com
Enter the keyword **Wisconsin**

INDEX

★ ★ ★

AUTHOR'S TIPS AND SOURCE NOTES

★ ★ ★

In writing this book, I've had a wealth of resources to call upon, not least the fact that I was born in Wisconsin and have lived there for much of my life. However, I also made a new trip from south to north through the state to remind myself of what I knew and to explore changes and spots I'd never seen before. I also had my own fount of information: a database of details about the various states, which I started compiling many years ago as an encyclopedia editor. Whenever I learned something intriguing—especially something not readily available in travel books or histories—I wrote it down on an index card.

Studying Native Americans, I found invaluable help from the classic *Atlas of the North American Indian*, by Carl Waldman, as well as *Prehistoric Indians of Wisconsin*, a publication of the Milwaukee Public Museum. Whenever I needed to check a fact, I knew I would find the answers in the Wisconsin State Historical Society publications, both online, and in *Wisconsin History Highlights: Delving into the Past*, written by Jonathan Kasparek, Bobbie Malone, and Erica Schock. Delightful cultural and local details often came from the always amazing Writers' Program book, *Wisconsin: A Guide to the Badger State*.

One of the great treasures of Wisconsin is the state historical society. It was founded in 1846, two years before Wisconsin became a state. The society has created an amazingly complete and easy-to-use Web site, with information, photos, historical newspaper articles, and bibliographies about Wisconsin, its people, its geography, and its history.